Clem Sunter

21st Century
Megatrends
Perspectives from a
FOX

HUMAN & ROUSSEAU / TAFELBERG

Published jointly by Human & Rosseau and Tafelberg,
both imprints of NB Publishers,
a division of Media24 Books (Pty) Ltd
Heerengracht 40, Cape Town 8001
South Africa

Commissioning Editor: Annie de Beer
Proofreader: Julie Miller
Checker: Lorraine Braid
Cover and book design by Nazli Jacobs
Set in Palatino
Printed and bound by Interpak Books,
Pietermaritzburg, South Africa

ISBN: 978-0-624-06605-7
ISBN: 978-0-624-06606-4 (epub)
ISBN: 978-0-624-06607-1 (mobi)

Product group from well-managed forests
and other controlled sources.

FSC
www.fsc.org
MIX
Paper from
responsible sources
FSC® C105735

Contents

Introduction

Think about how much life changes in a century, let alone a millennium. Our Victorian antecedents would have had no idea about how the car would change the way we live. Air travel would have been way beyond them. Phones they might have had an inkling about as the device was invented towards the end of the 19th century. Nevertheless, I doubt that they would have any grasp of so many aspects of our existence which we now take for granted. Of course, trains and ships, trade and wars, love and hate and many other things they would be familiar with.

So here we are at the beginning of the 21st century without much of a clue of what the world will be like at the beginning of the 22nd one. In the same manner as the original telephone did, the internet, the mobile and other late 20th century devices do provide some indications of the way the next two generations will evolve. However, we might be as surprised as the Victorians about some of the things we would encounter if we were around in the 2090s.

The title of this book, therefore, is not meant to imply that as a scenario planner I can look that far forward. It is more about identifying the forces shaping our lives for the next ten years which have become apparent since 2000. It is the subject of the first article of a set of weekly columns I have written for News24 between March 2012 and July 2013. The remainder cover a wide range of issues, but the theme of some of the most important ones is about how South Africa must establish an economic platform which will launch a new generation of entrepreneurs. Only by doing this will we make the rest of this century a prosperous one for all our citizens. Several also identify the red flags that we have to keep down to avoid a crash landing before a new economic model has kicked in.

I would like to thank Aneeqah Emeran at News24 who assists me every week in publishing my articles and Annie de Beer for the production of this book. I would also like to thank my colleague Chantell Ilbury for all the work she has done in making the 'mind of a fox' brand such a global success. The reason that a South African idea can break new ground in the field of strategic thinking is that we know – living on the African continent – that much of the future is uncertain and beyond our control. Like true foxes, South Africans invariably rise to the challenge of adapting to whatever the future throws at them. They have the resilience and spirit of innovation to thrive in the 21st century. All that is needed is leadership of the right kind.

Clem Sunter

21st century megatrends

Despite the unpredictability of the future, a competent scenario planner can identify certain major trends shaping it. Here is my best take.

Remember all these megatrends are beyond your control, so you must adapt to them. I have added an extra one since writing the article. We are entering a post-American world following the latest revelations about America's spying activities – even tapping the mobile phones of heads of state who are supposed to be allies. It shows a significant level of desperation and loss of leadership in the world's most powerful nation.

Not only has its relationship with the other G8 nations deteriorated, its influence among them has diminished. With the rise of China and other emerging economies, America's share of global GDP is declining. With its burgeoning national debt, its indebtedness to the rest of the world is growing. We are entering a leaderless world with increasing potential for conflict and unpleasant surprises.

Now that we are entering the 14th year of the current century, some of the megatrends shaping this century have become evident. As a 21st century fox, here is my top 10 list bearing in mind that these megatrends will apply for all global economic and political scenarios. In other words, they are universal rules of the game, not variables that may or may not come into play depending on which scenario you choose. I have also run them by my fellow fox, Chantell Ilbury.

1. Populations are ageing
One of the problems making the budget deficit of the US so difficult to solve is the extraordinary number of elderly people

who over the next 50 years will qualify for state-funded medical care and social security. Europe and Japan are in even more difficult situations given that the population is declining in numbers in countries like Italy and now Japan. China faces a demographic cliff in about 20 years time because of the one-child policy introduced in 1978 and, at this stage, the nation has very little in the way of pensions and medical cover for the elderly.

Of course, India, Africa, South America and Indonesia still have relatively young, growing populations where the challenge is to raise general living standards. Nevertheless, depending on the degree of success in achieving the latter objective, they too will one day face the same ageing problem as increasing longevity goes hand in hand with rising income levels. The number of people over 100 years old living on this planet is set to explode and somehow will have to be catered for.

2. More economies will return to a steady state

Japan has led the way. Having been a high growth economy for the 1970s and 1980s, it has had somewhere between zero and one percent annual growth since 1990. They have done everything to try and revive the economy and now have the highest national debt to GDP ratio in the world. Europe is about to follow suit, while America with its younger demographics will probably manage two percent per annum.

Growth, as a concept, has really only been around for 200 years. Prior to the industrial revolution and the massive increase in population in the 19th and 20th centuries, it was only the favoured few who expanded empires and trade. Now once again, we face a relatively flat economic universe driven by static populations in the more advanced economies.

3. We have moved from the Age of Knowledge to the Age of Intelligence

The internet now means that access to knowledge and facts has increased exponentially over the last 20 years. The differentiator now is the way we use the existing knowledge to create new knowledge and connect the dots by dreaming up ideas that have not been dreamt up before. This is all about intelligence which comes back to teaching children cognitive skills. In a steady state economic universe, the penalty for not having an intelligent strategy as a business is no longer slower sales growth than your competitors. It is death. Innovation has become an even more important element of a company's life cycle since to grow, somebody else has to shrink. Competition in being original has just undergone a quantum leap.

4. It is more about defending your wealth than growing your wealth

Since 2000, food price inflation has averaged around 10% a year. Petrol prices have climbed too. In fact, the only thing that has checked the rise in the consumer price index is property (and mortgages). Meanwhile, interest rates are at all-time lows and returns from most asset classes since the beginning of the century have been subdued. It is the classic squeeze particularly in Britain and Europe. It is thus becoming more difficult to make money with money unless you are prepared to take a higher risk of losing it. In fact, preserving the real value of your savings is now a stretch.

In a steady state universe, you have to be a value-driven investor intent on stocks offering a satisfactory dividend yield and modest price–earnings ratio. Put another way, you have to be a dog whisperer where you can tell the difference between the apparent dogs that offer the upside because they are priced cheaply on account of general market conditions and the real dogs that are cheap for a valid reason. All in all, the retirement age for the remainder of this century has risen to between 70 and 75. Even then, you will still need an intelligent financial adviser. Otherwise, it becomes a race between poverty and death.

5. Education is out of sync with the job market and changing nature of work

Around the world, youth unemployment is a real issue and in some countries has hit record highs. One of the principal reasons is that schools are educating pupils for the job market of the middle of the last century, not the one that exists now. In those days, a decent academic qualification guaranteed you a job. Nowadays most kids have to be entrepreneurs and start their own businesses. When will schools wake up to this megatrend? I don't know, but in the meantime society will have a significant propensity for social unrest among its young citizens. They are the first generation for whom life offers fewer opportunities than for their parents because of their inappropriate education.

6. We are witnessing a second scramble, and potentially more dangerous scramble, for resources

All the easy-to-find, easy-to-mine, easy-to-treat mineral and energy deposits have been found, mined and treated. We are now into the remoter deposits which require more infrastructure to get the product to the customer or more difficult deposits which require new methods of processing such as fracking. By the middle of this century this picture can only get worse which will signify that the next big technological wave after IT will be around improving resource utilisation efficiencies as well as making substitutes such as solar energy better-priced for the average consumer.

A growing scarcity of water and food is also developing which is why the Chinese are purchasing land in Africa and why nations on large rivers are beginning to be more aggressive about the way water is shared. Marine mining and offshore drilling are also being stepped up with nations quarrelling over ownership rights in places like the sea off China and Japan. Outright conflict cannot be ruled out.

7. Wars will continue to be fought as weapons become more sophisticated

This century has already seen its fair share of wars, but it is unlikely to have a war of the magnitude of the two world wars of the last century for one good reason: the principle of mutually assured destruction. Nukes have raised the stakes so much with their power of devastation that every nation, including America, will think twice about using them. Nevertheless, conventional weapons are being turned into weapons of mass destruction by improvements in technology as can be seen by the appalling destruction wrought by a single, deranged gunman in incidents in Norway and America. Missiles are longer-range, drones more accurate and explosives more deadly. While mankind's instinct to kill has in no way diminished, his ability to kill is forever improving. I doubt whether we will see a single month in this century where someone is not fighting a war somewhere in the world. Sad but true.

8. Like black swans, natural disasters will come out of the blue

Tsunamis, hurricanes, superstorms, earthquakes, volcanic eruptions and droughts will continue to take their toll. Mother Nature is beyond our control and, on account of a more populated world, can unleash events of increasing consequence for human life. Moreover, so far this century nothing serious has yet been done by the super-emitters on global warming. It hardly rates a mention among political leaders whose tenure of office is far more determined by their country's short-term economic performance than by long-term climate change. One hopes that the meticulous collection of further scientific data will put the theory beyond doubt. Consensus has never validated a hypothesis. Often it is one man like Einstein that advances science: but evidence is always the judge.

9. Dictatorial regimes will become rarer, but what replaces them is not necessarily democracy

One of the biggest phenomena of this century has been the trumping of tyranny in all the countries affected by the Arab Spring. However, it is too early to predict that democracy in the full sense of the word (constitutional rights, regular elections, limited presidential terms) is about to flower in the void left by old regimes. What is certain is that the social media combined with the internet and YouTube have irreversibly changed the balance of power in favour of the people. They can publish their gripes.

10. The work/life balance is now even more elusive

In the last century, young business executives did not work 24/7. They did not have mobile phones and could not get emails at home. They switched off at weekends and on holidays because nobody could reach them. Now work has intruded into every aspect of life. The strain is showing.

Eurowinked!

This article was written as a bit of a spoof on how European banks were asked to take a hit on their holdings of Greek bonds in order to prop up the Eurozone. I also wanted to highlight the danger of 'moral hazard', where you get seduced into taking a risk because you think part of that risk is laid off on other parties. If Greece had been a stand-alone nation, many of the banks would have seen the true risk of lending to it. However, as a member of an exclusive European club, Greece had access to the goodwill of the other members who were blind to its real weaknesses.

Overheard in an exclusive club in Frankfurt in Germany was this conversation between Angie, a woman of great influence, and Charles, the CEO of one of Germany's largest commercial banks. They were having coffee in the lounge after lunch. Angie is president of the club.

ANGIE: Charles, you need a haircut.

CHARLES: No I don't. I had one last week. You can see I have no hair on my neck.

ANGIE: I am not talking about that kind of haircut. You know George owes you one thousand Euro and he needs to repay you next week. Well, I want you to forgive 535 Euro of his debt and have him only pay you 465 Euro.

CHARLES: But then he is defaulting on his debt and I am going to lose more than half the credit I extended to him. That makes me especially angry as the rating agencies gave him a triple A.

ANGIE: Don't talk like that, Charles. You are going to volunteer to take a haircut on the money he owes you, shave the figure so to speak. Anyway, I know that you are probably insured for part of the loss.

CHARLES: Maybe, but why on earth should I do this?

ANGIE: Because we are a club, Charles, and I also know that you have been very generous and lent money to other members such as Peter, Sam and Ivan.

CHARLES: I must say they are all spendthrifts, lashing out on things they really don't need. I had the money and I felt sorry for them because they are people like us. They just fell on hard times. Besides which we have to put up a united front.

ANGIE: Precisely, and if people who are not members of this club get to hear that George unilaterally defaulted on his debt and created what I know you call a credit event, it would reflect badly on our collective image.

CHARLES: I see what you mean.

ANGIE: Moreover, it might mean that the world outside becomes harsher to Peter, Sam and Ivan. Then they might not be able to repay their loans either and your back pocket would receive an even bigger hit. Contagion can be nasty.

CHARLES: Gosh, I suppose I better take your advice.

ANGIE: However, I have one other favour to ask of you. Please would you roll over the 465 Euro and make it a new loan to George.

CHARLES: How will I know that I won't receive another haircut?

ANGIE: Just be a dear. George has promised to adjust his lifestyle and live within his means. The club must stick together.

CHARLES: What about you? Doesn't anybody in the club owe you any money?

ANGIE: Of course not. I'm not a banker and I don't have time to look after the interests of individual members. I just look after the finances of the club as a whole.

CHARLES: But you do need a haircut.

ANGIE: What do you mean?

CHARLES: It would make you look much younger!

Boots and all

The difference between World War I and World War II was that the first one laid the foundations for the second one with the poorly thought through and revengeful Treaty of Versailles. This allowed Adolf Hitler to rise from nowhere and exploit the economic misery of Germans in the aftermath. After the second war and learning from the first, the victors with initiatives like the Marshall Plan ensured that the losers were not resentful. Alas, in the case of many of the half-fought wars being fought now, the prospects for the countries concerned are not being improved by concerted measures to uplift the local citizenry when the intervention is over. There are no green shoots to turn the spring into summer and the problems remain.

I used to have lunch with my father at the Honourable Artillery Company (HAC) in Moorgate in the City of London. My father was a stockbroker and I was working at Anglo's London office in Holborn Viaduct. This was in the late 1960s before I moved to Africa.

At one lunch, we were joined by a senior army officer who served with my father during the World War II. The HAC, as it was known, was an elite artillery unit which did its bit in support of the infantry. During coffee, we were discussing whether the Allied carpet-bombing of Hamburg (called Operation Gomorrah) in July 1943 and of Dresden in February 1945 was necessary. As an idealistic young man, I condemned the attacks as unethical. I will never forget the answer from my father's friend.

He said: 'Half-fought wars are never won. You have to go in boots and all. Especially when the enemy does the same.

We can all express regret for the 65 000 civilian casualties caused by the firestorms that engulfed the two cities. But we had to wipe out every trace of the Nazis so that Germany could start afresh after the war was over. We had to demoralise the entire nation in order to make them think differently about Hitler. And, incidentally, he only took his own life when his bunker in Berlin was surrounded and he knew that he was finished.'

There is a ring of truth in what he said all those years ago. Germany, totally stripped of Nazism, has ascended to the top spot in Europe and has even overtaken its old foe, Britain. One could apply the same logic to Japan. The dropping of the two atom bombs in August, 1945, one on Hiroshima and the second on Nagasaki, ended the war in a decisive manner with a clear winner and loser. Japan, stripped of imperialistic ambition, mirrored Germany in its astonishing economic recovery which meant that, until recently overtaken by China, it was the second largest economy in the world.

The third example is an interesting one because it is America itself. People forget how vicious the Civil War that ended in the defeat of the Confederacy in 1865 was. Major General Sherman (after whom the tank is named) invented the strategy of total war by marching his Yankee troops through Atlanta to the sea, destroying all the infrastructure, buildings and farms along the way. After the surrender of General Lee in April 1865, America never looked back. With its territorial integrity preserved, with slavery abolished and with an effective reconstruction programme in place, the economy enjoyed such a boom that the US assumed pole position in the world in a matter of decades.

Before getting to the point of this chapter, let us look at the outcome of three half-fought wars. The Korean War (1950–53) was one where the Soviet Union and China supported the North and America and its allies the South. After the last two years ended in military stalemate, an armistice was declared and Korea was split into two portions along the Demilitarized Zone. To this day, the North and the South have an uneasy relationship punctuated with an occasional incident. The South has done well economically, while the North has only its army and a few nuclear weapons to show it has progressed.

The Vietnam War lasted from 1955 to 1975 with America trying to prevent a communist takeover of South Vietnam. Following the capture of Saigon by the Vietnam People's Army in 1975 and the simultaneous departure of American troops, America failed in its objective despite overwhelming logistical superiority. Vietnam was reunified in 1976 and has since put in a pretty decent performance in uplifting its population.

The Iraq War (2003–2011) did end up with the defeat of Saddam Hussein and American soldiers did leave in December 2011. However, it is too early to say that sectarian violence is a thing of the past and that Sunni and Shia Arabs are going to forge a constructive relationship with one another. Car bombs still go off in crowded markets and the place could still descend into civil war.

Now my point. We have one half-fought war continuing in Afghanistan and another one which could be half-fought or fully fought about to erupt in Iran. In the former case, both America and Britain have announced total troop withdrawals in 2014. My prediction, based on the assertion of my father's friend and the examples of half-fought wars quoted, is that very little is going to change. The Taliban will be back and if Vietnam is anything to go by, they may well take charge once again. Will it all have been worth it? That will be a question which will frequently be asked behind the scenes (not in public of course).

A conflict in Iran is still to come and will only take place in the event that the nuclear issue cannot be resolved peacefully.

The stakes are much higher because, like Syria, America and its allies are on one side and Russia, together with China, are on the other side. It could be a war by proxy. Equally, though, Israel could precipitate things as a result of the threats made to its existence by the Iranian leadership. Again, based on the analysis in this chapter, the issue will only be resolved one way or another by a war without limits. A half-hearted affair will achieve nothing.

My conclusion is that war is digital: you either have to go in boots and all or not at all. Success is compromised by anything in between. One therefore has to be far more cautious about going to war in circumstances where the enemy does not pose a direct threat to your survival. Leave well alone and don't interfere. Keep your nose out. For the record, neither Korea nor Vietnam nor Iraq nor Afghanistan constituted a direct threat to America. Japan did in 1941 and so did Germany to Britain in 1939. Self-preservation meant no constraints other than the Geneva Convention. The enemy was crushed. A new chapter began in 1945.

Yet, it can still be convincingly argued that, considering the act in itself, the bombing of Hamburg and Dresden represented the cold-blooded murder of civilians on a massive scale. It could not be justified even as a retaliatory act for the bombing of London and Coventry. Two wrongs don't make a right. Thus, war remains one of the most difficult topics to discuss and arrive at a reasonable answer.

Keeping the red flags down

Classical scenario planning techniques focus on the quality and content of the scenarios themselves, sometimes with endless iterations. In our case, we put as much effort into identifying the flags which would suggest that you are moving from one scenario to another. Then, based on whether the flags are rising or falling, we attach a subjective probability to each scenario. Now comes the most important part. Based on the probability and impact of each scenario, you weigh up your options and decide whether you are going to do something now to cope with its challenges; or have a contingency plan in case its probability increases. Either way, you are trying to copy the agility of a fox.

There are two reasons why Chantell Ilbury and I provide red flags for downside scenarios. The first is to allow people time to take action on their own behalf to ameliorate the impact of such scenarios on their organisations or personal lives. The second is to give them the chance, collectively with other people, to keep the red flags down in order to minimise the probability of Armageddon-type scenarios becoming reality.

Such is the case with our most negative scenario for South Africa which we call "Failed State"

It is where we join the likes of Somalia, Afghanistan and Syria because the level of violence and unpredictability surrounding our future rises to a point where foreigners are too afraid to come here, let alone invest in any new business. Yet again we are isolated from the rest of the world, but this time not as a result of sanctions but through being perceived as too high a risk.

We have four red flags and one tendency associated with

the "Failed State" scenario. A tendency is like Japan being located in a seismically active zone of the earth's crust, so it has a higher probability of earthquakes. At the moment, we attach low odds to the "Failed State" scenario. But if any of the four flags rise or the tendency turns into reality, watch out – the odds are increasing and it is time to seek protection.

Actions of the first kind in the first paragraph are to keep your passport up to date; possibly look for a job overseas; take as much of your wealth offshore as you are legally allowed to do; and if you own a business expand the geographical footprint elsewhere in Africa and overseas. In a "Failed State" scenario, the rand could fall to 100 against the US dollar (after all it has devalued by a factor of ten since 1980).

Nevertheless, being patriotic, it is actions of the second kind which hold more interest for Chantell and myself. Let me therefore list the flags and tendencies and provide the counter-measures to keep them down and out of play.

The first red flag is nationalisation as many of our trading partners would regard it as a retrogressive step of the worst possible kind. The policy has failed miserably in most of the countries where it has been implemented and anyway the question universally asked is: How on earth would the government afford to pay fair value for the mines and the banks? It would push our national debt to GDP ratio from its current modest level to something approaching that of Greece. Not paying fair value on the other hand is tantamount to confiscation which would be a total turn-off for foreign investors.

The ANC appears to have arrived at a similar conclusion so this flag is down at present. But the best way to keep it there is for the mining companies and banks to initiate major employee share ownership programmes. The capital of this country would not be shared with government but with the workers. It would no longer be perceived as monopoly capital.

The second red flag is a clumsy implementation of national

health insurance which leads to a decline in the quality of private medical care. This could cause another mass exodus of skills, since young talented people in particular put a high premium on access to decent health care for themselves and their families. The way to keep this flag down is for the major private sector health care players to offer to go into partnership with the government with regard to the management of the big state hospitals. Thus, a stampede towards the private hospitals can be avoided when the public have freedom of choice on where to go for medical care.

The third red flag is a media tribunal with punitive powers. This flag has partially risen with the passing of the secrecy bill. Muzzling the media is as bad as undermining the independence of the judiciary. It can precipitate a quantum leap in corruption as there is no longer the fear of exposure. The way to keep this flag down is to campaign for a very narrow definition of a secret, preferably only military ones.

The fourth red flag is potentially the most toxic and lethal—land grabs. The latter could even be the trigger for a civil war in South Africa. Already the fear of this flag rising has caused the number of commercial farmers to diminish and constrained new investment. This flag will only be kept down by bringing all the major players in agriculture together in an Agridesa (i.e. an agricultural equivalent of a Codesa) to negotiate a land reform programme with a reasonable chance of success.

The tendency arises from the three characteristics shared by all the Arab countries that have gone through the Arab Spring: abnormally high youth unemployment; a growing alienation from society by those unemployed young people; and active social networks. South Africa has all three factors which means our own version of the Arab Spring could be only one random event away. Measures to stop this tendency turning into reality may include tax incentives for companies to take on young recruits out of school and train them; an easing of labour laws for small business to give them the flexibility to employ extra staff; teaching pupils entrepreneurial skills as part of the curriculum; and some form of national community service.

By articulating the "Failed State" scenario as a low probability, high impact event – what Nassim Taleb refers to as a Black Swan – Chantell and I hope that we have provided an adequate motivation for everybody to take action to keep the red flags down.

Einstein was right about Israel

I wish Israel's politicians had the wisdom of Einstein and could instigate a low-key initiative along the lines that Einstein suggested. No big names, just ordinary people reaching out to one another.

We normally associate Albert Einstein's name with the advancement of physics, in particular the special theory and general theory of relativity. We do not think of him as being astute in political matters; but I came across an article by Donald McIntyre that was recently published in the *Cape Times* and *The Independent* which suggests otherwise.

In a letter written to the Arab editor of the newspaper *Falastin* in December 1929, Einstein stated: 'I think the two great Semitic peoples that have made each in its own way lasting contributions to the civilisation of the modern Western world can have a great future in common and that instead of facing each other with unfruitful hostility and mutual distrust they should seek for the possibility for sympathetic co-operation.'

The following year, he outlined the process to achieve this objective, a central part of which would be the establishment of two teams of four members, one side Jewish, the other Arab, that would act as a bargaining council. Neither side would have any politicians in their ranks. Rather, he suggested a physician, jurist, worker representative and cleric. Their meetings would be confidential, but when three on each side agreed to a resolution, it could be made public. In this way, the council would 'lead to a state in which differences will gradually be eliminated and common representation of the interests of the country will be upheld.'

Brilliant. Only a couple of months ago, I was talking to a

prominent member of the Jewish community in South Africa and, without knowing anything about Einstein's recommendations, we both agreed this was the only way forward. What was needed was a negotiating forum to kick-start the same kind of process that occurred in the early 1990s in South Africa when everybody said that the two sides would never meet. They did and, even though on several occasions the parties walked away as a result of a breakdown in talks, the deal came together.

I know that roadmaps on peace in the Middle East have already been constructed, handshakes between leaders have taken place and agreements have been signed. Tragically, progress has stalled and somehow we are almost back to square one. Hence, the need for a new initiative; and, rather than involving the politicians with entrenched interests, bring in a representative panel of experts from both sides – university professors and the like – to restart the dialogue. Again the entire conversation should be held in private as Einstein suggested so that grandstanding is avoided.

McIntyre quotes Professor Hanoch Gutfreund at the end of his article. He is an eminent theoretical physicist himself and academic head of the Einstein archive. While calling Einstein's proposal naïve , he added: 'It's great, it's romantic, it's beautiful and maybe one day if nothing else works this is the only way to go about it.' Well, that day has arrived.

Active learning

In life, only a handful of people influence your powers of reasoning significantly. In my case, two people stand out. The philosopher, Anthony Quinton and the legendary scenario planner, Pierre Wack. They both taught me that the only way to advance your knowledge is to develop a way of looking at the external world which is ready for the unexpected. We all have filters in our perception caused by our background, emotional make-up, likes and dislikes and the trick is to compensate for them in order to arrive at a picture as close to the truth as possible.

According to one definition, a lecture is an efficient way of transferring notes from the lecturer's to the student's notebook without passing through the head of either body. Obviously, this definition was in the mind of the inventors of 'active learning' where much more attention is given to the learner being actively involved in the process of his own learning.

I was introduced to the concept at a fascinating pair of workshops held in Johannesburg and Cape Town to which I was asked to make a contribution. They were organised by the LR Management Group (LRMG), but had heavy input from the Harvard Business School (HBS) with which LRMG has close links. JF Goldstyn, Director of Harvard Business Publishing, made the observation that active learning could overthrow the style of teaching that has ruled universities for over 600 years.

Indeed, there are now senior executive development programmes at HBS which are only 10% formal learning and 90% informal learning. The majority of the course is staged around learning events involving a degree of online learning, peer learning, social media and improving the ability of spontaneous learning on the job. In other words, you do it yourself and through interaction in teams. You are your own leader.

I can relate to this because at university I remember bunking many of the formal lectures and preferring to go to the library to read the books and articles I selected to read. In addition, I had a one-on-one tutorial once a week with one of England's greatest philosophers at the time, a man called Anthony Quinton. He preferred to have a conversation about topics which at times were far removed from the formal syllabus. However, it taught me so much more about putting whatever cognitive skills I possessed to maximum use than having him pass information to me on how my essays could be improved. I reckon the weekly debate with him did more than anything else to set me up for the career I subsequently pursued and not to accept anything at face value. It taught me to argue logically and crucially to give up when the other side offered a better argument.

Moreover, Quinton opened my eyes to experimentation with seemingly ridiculous ideas that might have a grain of truth on further analysis. 'Never let the fear of being the laughing stock deter you from breaking new ground', he used to say. Sometimes, when we reached deadlock on a philosophical point, he would throw his hands in the air and say that truth had many different faces, and compromise was the answer. One of his favourite quotes was: 'Occasionally, the Catholic Church has to go to the Moulin Rouge.'

So, it is exciting to see institutions like Harvard have come to the same view about the advantages of active learning that I, probably using a different phrase, came to all those years ago. Furthermore, in this day and age of smart gadgets and the internet, a learner is much more empowered to seek knowledge and truth for himself and herself – from infancy onwards.

I wonder what the course content of universities and business schools will be like in 600 years time. Maybe students will teach and professors will learn!

And the Oscar of all time goes to . . .

I now have to add Daniel Day-Lewis to my short list for his amazing portrayal of Abraham Lincoln using the skills of a prairie lawyer to push through the 13th Amendment to the US Constitution abolishing slavery, just before his assassination in April 1865.

I love conversations around likes and dislikes because we are all different and that is what makes the world go around. Favourites of mine are pet hates of yours and vice versa. One of the reasons a democracy works is that we vote for different parties and leaders. What's more, we occasionally change our minds. The person we had no time for yesterday suddenly becomes a bosom buddy tomorrow.

So the other day when the topic at a business dinner for which I was the guest speaker turned to the arts and choice of best actor ever male or female, I was hooked. Of course, Meryl Streep was suggested for a variety of roles and the versatility of moving from being the star of *Mama Mia* to *The Iron Lady*. Helen Mirren for her portrayal of Queen Elizabeth II was also nominated. Among male actors Marlon Brando as *The Godfather* and for his magic performance in the movie *On The Waterfront* in 1954 got the nod. We all agreed he was the James Dean who could act.

Probably the person around whom the majority converged in their opinion was Al Pacino and particularly for playing the blind, retired army officer in *Scent of a Woman* in 1993. Who will forget Lieutenant Colonel Frank Slade as he whisked a young woman around the dance floor or drove a Ferrari around the city streets with little or no attention to instructions? He really did come across as blind in the film but that is what good acting is all about – convincing the audience you are the part you play.

I guess I showed my age because the Oscar of all Oscars for me goes to a young lady who mesmerised me for 3 hours and 44 minutes in the most famous picture of all time – *Gone with the Wind* – about the American Civil War and its aftermath in the South. The name of the actress is Vivien Leigh and she played the wilful and sometimes downright mischievous Scarlett O' Hara opposite Clark Gable's hedonistic but likeable character of Rhett Butler. She was only given the part a month before shooting began at the beginning of 1939 and, being the daughter of a British officer in the Indian Cavalry, she had a few weeks in which to perfect the accent of a southern belle.

She won the Oscar as leading lady but Clark Gable failed to do so as leading man. The most famous line in the movie came at the end when he walked out on her into the mist: 'Frankly, my dear, I don't give a damn.' In real terms, *Gone with the Wind* is the highest grossing film in the history of cinema beating *Titanic* and all others. Sadly, three of the four leading members of the cast died in their 50s: Leigh herself after a long bout of ill-health including tuberculosis and bi-polar disorder; Gable and Leslie Howard who was cast as Ashley Wilkes, the great, unrequited love of Scarlett, in the film. Only Olivia de Havilland, who played Melanie married to Ashley, survives in her mid 90s.

As a final twist, Leigh was married for 20 years to the man that many people in Britain would vote as the greatest actor of all time: Sir Laurence Olivier. During the making of *Gone with the Wind*, she missed Olivier every day as he was the real love of her life. Like Richard Burton and Liz Taylor, their marriage was dramatic too. The curtain came down on it in 1960 and seven years later she died.

Animal spirits

I hope this chapter proves now and forever that the future, and particularly markets for shares and commodities, cannot be reduced to a mathematical model. Intuition is the key.

I've only just realised what a genius John Maynard Keynes really was. I was watching an interview of Alan Greenspan, ex-chairman of the US Federal Reserve Bank, on Bloomberg. He was asked what his forecast for the US economy over the next six months might be. He replied that he was beginning to believe Keynes' words on animal spirits and that you had to use behavioural science to say anything about the US economy.

So I looked up the words of Keynes on the internet as he is considered the greatest British economist of the last century. This is what he said in *The General Theory of Employment, Interest and Money*, generally regarded as his masterpiece and published in 1936.

'Most, probably, of our decisions to do something positive, the full consequences of which will be drawn out over many days to come, can only be taken as a result of animal spirits – of a spontaneous urge to action rather than inaction and not as the outcome of a weighted average of quantitative benefits multiplied by quantitative probabilities.

Thus if the animal spirits are dimmed and the spontaneous optimism falters, leaving us to depend on nothing but a mathematical expectation, enterprise will fade and die.'

Elsewhere he said: 'Individual initiative will only be adequate when reasonable calculation is supplemented and supported by animal spirits, so that the thought of ultimate loss which often overtakes pioneers, as experience undoubtedly tells us and them, is put aside as a healthy man puts aside the expectation of death.'

There are two very different groups to whom I would like to read out these quotes. The first is the government here and, in particular, our President as well as the two ministers most closely associated with the development of our economy – Trevor Manuel and Ebrahim Patel. My questions to them would be: 'Are you taking the advice of Keynes and doing everything to kindle the animal spirits of our present and future entrepreneurs? Is the raising of the next generation of South African industrialists foremost in your mind? What are you doing to create an environment in which these animal spirits are not dimmed by regulation but are allowed to roam free?'

The second group is across the ocean in America. The foxy methodology is increasingly being used by organisations there wishing to have an intense conversation about adapting their strategy to the extraordinary times we live in. One of the questions I am asked over and over again by institutions like MIT is what kind of mathematical model underpins the way we link the flags to the scenarios so that one can assign accurate probabilities to them. The answer is that we have none and prefer to use instinct and feel. Our probabilities are subjective and therefore open to debate.

I can now buttress our side of the argument by mentioning not only that the future only happens once, which makes it impossible to quantify the odds precisely on a particular scenario. I can now, in addition, invoke Keynes and his point that most innovative action derives from animal spirits and spontaneous urges rather than rational analysis.

I can end my address to both groups with the quip that foxes are animals with huge spirits. The best way to handle the future is to behave like one!

The lesson of Trafalgar

Nothing beats knowledge of the game when it comes to the selection of leaders in any field. Charisma without knowledge and a sense of morality can be very dangerous. Lord Nelson had all three.

The reason England beat France and Spain combined at the naval battle of Trafalgar in October 1805 is simple. Lord Nelson and the captains of the fleet he commanded had plenty of years of sea experience under their belts; whereas the French and Spanish top naval officers were chosen from the aristocracy, some of whom had had no time at sea at all. The English commanders were professional: the French and Spanish commanders were amateurs.

For exactly the same reason, if you look at the managers of virtually any sports team – be it rugby, cricket, soccer, golf, tennis or hockey – they have virtually all played the sport themselves as professionals and understand every aspect of the game. Their knowledge is built up over years of successes and failures and being au fait with all the other players and sides in the game. There no such thing as instant wisdom in sport.

In business, the identical principle applies. The best CEOs are the ones that have come up through the ranks and know the ins and outs of most of the jobs down the line. They have walked the job for years and have immediate empathy with their employees. They can put themselves into the shoes of their staff and customers and thereby anticipate their needs. Equally, they can think strategically and select the best tactics because the game they are in is in their blood. During their years at work, they will have gained the financial instinct which tells them what are good bets and bad bets in terms of projects and deals.

In education, the best principals are the ones who have sniffed the chalk on the blackboard and participated in the dynamics of the classroom – in other words they have been teachers themselves. They can tell the difference between a good and bad teacher a mile away. They put their heart and soul into improving the intellectual potential and life skills of the young people under their control.

With NGOs, the best directors are the ones who are regarded as champions in their field, tirelessly fighting for better conditions for the communities and the individuals they serve. Over time, they have developed close relationships with their major donors such that real trust binds the two parties. Trust never comes overnight. It always takes time.

The bottom line is that with leadership of any organisation, a primary requisite is professionalism. That can only be gained through experience combined with ethical standards which are never compromised. This would suggest that the leadership of every single parastatal in South Africa, every single municipality, every single hospital, the police, the justice system, the ports and harbours, all other infrastructure and all development agencies should be chosen on one single criterion: a thorough knowledge of the game and excellent performance in it over many years. In most cases, this means promotion from within.

Parachuting amateurs in for whatever reason – connections, gratitude for other work, nice guys that think in a similar vein – will result in the same thing that happened to the French and Spanish at Trafalgar. Defeat.

England's premier asset

Without Sir Alex Ferguson, the Premier League will never be quite the same again. He was the most successful manager in the history of the Premier League, winning more trophies than anyone else. I will miss him chewing gum on the sideline to keep his emotions under control!

If it had been the script for a play, it would not have been believed. Manchester United at the final whistle of their game were technically champions, and then Manchester City scored those two goals in injury time to pip them. What a crazy finish to a crazy season. Sergio Aguero's shot changed the lives of millions of fans around the world in the blink of a second – and his own as well!

Why is England's Premier League the number one sporting league in the world with no rival in any other country? Why does it attract the biggest global audience and have the widest geographical footprint? There are eight reasons:

1 **Soccer is the beautiful game.** Lovers of other sports hate it but no other game attracts the imagination of the masses like soccer. Every little boy growing up in the back streets of forgotten slums surrounding major cities in England, Europe, Africa and South America dreams of being a soccer star. Moreover, the game in England is more free-flowing and energetic than it is on the continent. The average Premier League player covers 14km in one match.

2 **The Premier League is open to the best players in the world.** If there is any example of what a liberal immigration policy can do for a country, it is the fact that the

Premier League has probably the best collection of players from all over the world. African stars feature prominently in most of the top teams, including Didier Drogba in mine – Chelsea.

3 **Rich foreigners have provided financial backing to many of the clubs.** Americans, Arabs and Russians have put in sufficient cash to lure the talent. A good player gets ±£100 000 per match or ±£3.8m for the season. That is around R50m per annum. The superstars get double that.

4 **Every match is televised.** Nothing exhibits the power of television more than the fact that in virtually every restaurant and pub the world over, you can watch the game and analysis from experts.

5 **Each club is heavily branded.** You can buy shirts, caps and all the other paraphernalia of any of the clubs. Walk into any mall in South Africa and you will see someone in the colours of one of the Premier League clubs.

6 **Most of the clubs have been around for 120 years or more.** This means that the brand of the club is more important than that of the individual player. Hence players come and go, but loyalty of the fans remains with the club.

7 **The crowd are fanatic at matches.** It makes all the difference to have an enthusiastic audience. Nothing depresses more than empty stands.

8 **The manager and coaching squads are brilliant.** Again many managers are not English but they are all as important to the success of the Premier League as the players. Each has his own personality which comes across in the post-match interviews.

All these points suggest that one of the most strategic decisions ever taken in sport happened 20 years ago when England's First Division was converted into the Premier League. It is the country's premier asset.

Entrepreneurs in chains

I now have an ally in Barack Obama who, on his recent visit to South Africa, emphasised the role of entrepreneurs in keeping us at the head of the economic game in Africa. When will we ever learn that freedom is not working for somebody else? It is working for yourself and climbing the ladder of your own choice.

This chapter is prompted by two conversations I have had recently; one with a young Chinese woman at a lunch with friends last Sunday and the other with a South African businessman who has just returned from Lagos in Nigeria.

In the first conversation, the lady said that despite the strong political hold that the Chinese Communist Party has over the nation, in the minor towns and villages across the country economic anarchy reigns. This has been incredibly beneficial in that it has led to an entrepreneurial revolution which has propelled China to No 2 in the global economic order behind the US. It may not be the sole cause because you have to consider foreign investment in China as well, but sure as night follows day it has helped.

The businessman said that he had gone to Lagos expecting another down-at-heel, demotivated Third World city. Instead, he discovered one of the most exciting places he has ever visited, putting it on the same pedestal as Hong Kong. He found the entrepreneurial energy irresistible in Lagos. Everywhere he went people were buying and selling things in an unregulated environment other than the prime rule of cash on delivery. He now considers Johannesburg's boastful slogan of being the leading business centre in Africa to be totally empty. He sees the future of African capitalism as

Lagos. Johannesburg belongs to the history book of colonial capitalism.

What both these people's opinions had in common was the idea of economic freedom – not the one peddled by Julius Malema of transferring assets at no cost between rich and poor with an increasing role for the state. The one they have in mind is breaking the oppressive chains binding the small business owners in this country. True liberation will only come when all those creative souls who are not politicians, not civil servants, not directors or employees of large, established businesses, not unionists or union members, not the recipients of regular monthly pay cheques, are put on a par with those inhabiting parliament and the formal economy.

Consider the following chains that currently shackle South African entrepreneurs:

1 The snobbish attitude of the political and business intelligentsia in this country which at worst consider entrepreneurs to be criminals and at best greedy little capitalists that need to be tolerated as a sideshow. Whichever, they have to be regulated as an irresponsible underclass.

2 All recent national plans. They have emphasised the developmental state which is a euphemism for more chains and more regulation and more economic prioritisation. The people writing these plans have never personally had to create wealth themselves in order to be paid. As recipients of regular salaries, they have no idea of the risks involved in being an entrepreneur. Remember it is economic anarchy in China which has largely contributed to its economic miracle. Nassim Taleb puts it a different way in his books about black swans and randomness: it is all a matter of luck as to which businesses grow into major international concerns and which fail. The best policy is thus to have an environment which maximises

the number of new businesses without any preferences for particular industries. The lucky ones will make it and you have no idea beforehand which they are.

3 The vast bureaucracy surrounding the establishment and ongoing operation of a small business in a legal manner. We are now regarded as one of the most hostile countries in the world for entrepreneurs. Most small businesses here only have one employee – the owner. The reason is that nobody wants to take on extra people with the potential hassle of going to the labour court if these people fail to perform. Below a certain size, entrepreneurs should have total freedom to hire and fire as it is their business and their money after all. It is not the taxpayers' money.

4 The culture of non-payment to small business which thrives in the world of big business and government. In big business, standard payment terms can extend to 120 days while some state entities like hospitals never pay which is why they are in such trouble. The whole process of being approved as a vendor is now used as an excuse to defer payment. Can you imagine going to a supermarket and walking out with a trolley full of goods and saying to the security guard that you will pay as soon as the supermarket fills in the appropriate forms to become your approved vendor? Big companies do this all the time to small service providers.

5 The tight-fisted approach of all providers of capital to entrepreneurs in South Africa. The financial universe here resembles a well-heeled club that is happy to extend credit to members. But woe betide uppity non-members who rudely knock on its doors making unreasonable requests to finance small business ventures. What a lack of manners! Why don't they just disappear and borrow from their equally vulgar and impecunious friends?

I can go on, but we have completely lost the plot. Until we fundamentally change our mindset with regard to entrepreneurs and regard them as the centrepiece of this nation's future economic prosperity, we are finished. Nigeria will overtake us in the next 10 years as the continent's largest and most vibrant economy and leave us eating dust.

Beam me up Muskie

Someone should produce a comprehensive list of all the South Africans who live in other countries and are heroes in these countries. I would include all those who were born here but who are no longer citizens here. Then we might realise what an exceptional contribution has been made to the history of mankind by all those inside and outside of our borders who share one characteristic: they are part of the greater South African family.

Yet again the South African media has failed to headline an amazing first by somebody who hails from South Africa. Yes, there are articles but you have to dig for them in the middle pages. They still believe that only bad news sells newspapers here.

The hero of the moment is Elon Musk, raised in Pretoria by a South African father and Canadian-American mother. He matriculated from Pretoria Boys High School in 1988 when he was 17, having taught himself to program a computer and developed a space game called Blastar at the age of 12.

He is now a billionaire, having founded Space X, Tesla Motors which makes electronic cars and Paypal, an online payment system which is now part of eBay. Space X has just launched the Falcon 9 rocket with the intention of having its Dragon capsule dock with the International Space Station, thereby providing nearly half a ton of food, clothing and laboratory kit. Setting off from Cape Canaveral in Florida, this is the first commercial space flight by a private company in the history of mankind.

Musk tweeted on his page: 'Falcon flew perfectly! Dragon in orbit, comm locked and solar arrays active.' He added:

'Feels like a giant weight just came off my back.' John Holdren, chief science adviser to Barack Obama, said: 'Every launch into space is a thrilling event, but this one is especially exciting because it represents the potential of a new era in American space flight.'

Musk has received congratulations from people all over America including senators and congressmen and even rival organisations like Virgin whose founder Richard Branson has similar space ambitions to Musk.

Like Siyabulela Xuza who has a minor planet named after him by NASA for his rocket fuel and who is now studying at Harvard University, Musk has become a superstar in America. It speaks volumes about the difference between American and South African culture. Americans celebrate individual excellence no matter where it comes from. It looks for the heroes of the future. We tolerate mediocrity and celebrate only heroes of the past.

The latest global economic scenarios

We are not out of the woods yet. Our scenario with the highest odds of 40% remains "Hard Times" with the world remaining uniformly flat in economic terms for the foreseeable future. Equally, the two-speed "Ultraviolet" scenario – where growth in the New World economies outperforms that in the Old World economies by a factor of 3:1 – still has a 30% probability. In this scenario, the younger demographic profile of the New World acts as an accelerator versus the ageing demographic profile of the Old World acting as a brake. China remains the key flag to watch. We retain our anxiety about its banking system, in addition to which we are now beginning to worry about it becoming more expensive in its production costs. This will necessitate a move from cheap replication of Western ideas to innovation and completely new products, a transition that Japan made in the 1970s. Will China rise to this challenge? We are not sure and it is the reason why we slightly favour "Hard Times" for everybody.

As far as the two outsiders are concerned – the "Forked Lightning" of a second crash and the "New Balls Please" of a full recovery creating another boom albeit of a completely different nature – we now split the odds at 15% each. Quantitative easing by the principal central banks is keeping interest rates on government debt down, thus reducing the risk of national default; and unemployment in America is falling towards the critical level of 6.5% which will inspire confidence that a proper but slow recovery is in place.

There you have it. Don't bet on a single future. Rather keep all four of our possible futures in mind, watch the flags go up or down, adjust the probabilities and adapt your strategies and tactics as you go along. More and more companies are agreeing with the greater flexibility inherent in our approach when faced with these volatile times.

Eleven years ago Chantell Ilbury and I co-authored a book called *The Mind of a Fox*. In it we said that much of the future is beyond your control and is uncertain. The only way to handle it is to play different scenarios, examine their probability and impact and look at the options to seize the opportunities offered in each scenario and counter the threats.

Before the Great Financial Crash of 2008 the majority of companies preferred to base their strategy on a single, expertly-driven forecast. Now they are not so sure and are much more willing to interrogate their vision and strategy by measuring the resilience of both against a variety of scenarios. In particular, they are prepared to change the fundamental direction of the business should a case be made for doing so.

Hard Times

What are we now telling our clients about the possibilities for the global economy? The first scenario we call "Hard Times" for at least the next five years. It is a flat-line future of minimal economic growth for the world as a whole. Essentially, it is the Japanese experience for the last 22 years despite that country implementing easy-money policies throughout the period and attaining the highest national debt to GDP ratio of any country anywhere (210% of GDP against a recommended maximum of 60%). Japan has averaged 1% p.a. economic growth compared to 8% p.a. in the 1970s and 1980s. The Nikkei stock index is now below 9 000 compared to nearly 40 000 in December 1989.

In the "Hard Times" scenario, companies with intelligent strategies will continue to grow but companies with mediocre strategies will go to the wall. Value for money and the cheaper alternative are the key drivers of consumer behaviour, so companies that reflect this trend in their product offering will do well.

Ultraviolet

The second mainline scenario we offer is called "Ultraviolet". It is where the Old World economies go through the five year 'U' while the New World economies experience a 'V' like recovery and grow at least three times faster than their Old World colleagues. In other words, we live in a two-speed 'UV' world where the principal strategy for multinational companies is to chase the 'V'. For many American and European companies it is their favourite scenario. Accordingly they are doing everything they can to establish a presence in China, India, Africa and South America.

Our principal flag for choosing between "Hard Times" and "Ultraviolet" is China's future economic growth rate. If it remains in the range of 8–10% p.a. then all the countries supplying China with resources will continue to do well in China's slipstream. If, however, China has the kind of wobble that Japan had at the end of 1989, then everybody is condemned to "Hard Times". We have gone more negative on China for two reasons: exports constitute 38% of China's GDP and exporting into a flat Europe does China's growth prospects no good; and in major cities outside of Beijing and Shanghai there are large numbers of unoccupied suburbs where municipalities have borrowed the money to build them from Chinese banks. These loans could go bad and trigger a banking crisis in China.

Accordingly, we give a 40% subjective probability to "Hard Times" during the next five years and 30% to "Ultraviolet". Like two racehorses leading the field but with not much distance between them, they are jockeying for prime position. Watching the data coming out of China on its economy is thus a continuous activity. Of course, you can bet on both scenarios by offering value for money and chasing the 'V' at the same time.

47

New Balls Please

We would not be good futurists if we did not explore the outer limits of the cone of uncertainty that opens up into the future. We have two scenarios which we call 'outsiders', but for which Malcolm Gladwell would prefer the term 'outliers'. The first is an extremely positive one where Ben Bernanke's policy of almost zero interest rates works for the US – the world's largest economy. It fully recovers next year and drags the whole world up with it in a full-scale 'V'. The title of this scenario is "New Balls Please", a Wimbledon expression to signify the players are getting new tennis balls because it is a new set.

We feel the recovery will usher in a completely different game for which new balls are needed in two important respects. Firstly, the East will be the economic equivalent to the West, thereby overturning several centuries of Western supremacy. Marketing strategies of companies will need to accommodate this. Secondly, the world is finally running out of resources and there is no Planet B. With rising population numbers and a widespread economic recovery, resource prices will go through the roof – oil possibly reaching $500 a barrel. One statistic says it all: if China ever mirrors American standards of living we would need four planets (which we have not got).

Technologies which improve the efficiency of resource consumption, particularly oil and metals, will be the most sought after as will substitutes like solar energy. More efficient supply chains which reduce the freight cost element in the final price of a product will also be a precondition for competitiveness. Our lifestyle will probably change whereby shopping at local neighbourhood stores will be preferable to travelling to distant malls. Localisation will replace globalisation.

At the moment, we only assign a 10% probability to this scenario as the two flags which would indicate it is in play are down: a drop in the US unemployment rate to around 7% (it has come down from 9.5% to 8.3% but still has a way to go); and a levelling-off or reduction in the national debt to GDP ratios of the Old World economies to indicate that governments are finally getting their financial affairs in order. Obviously, the best strategy in this scenario is to invest in resource businesses (like farming, water, mining and energy) as well as renewable alternatives to fossil fuels.

Forked Lightning

The last scenario we put forward is the one we most fear: a double dip where the worst is yet to come. We call it "Forked Lightning". There is a parallel: 1932. Everyone talks about the Wall Street Crash of 1929. In actual fact, the market went down in 1929, recovered in 1930 and 1931 and then crashed to 11% of its peak value in 1932. The equivalent today would be the Dow Jones Industrial Average free-falling from its current level of 12 500 to 1 500 which would be a catastrophe. We have two flags for this scenario. The first one is a sudden jump in the interest rate on US 10 year treasury bonds to somewhere between 4 and 5%. This would indicate a loss of faith in the way America is handling its budget deficit. Right now this flag is down as the interest rate is below 2% since most investors prefer American to European paper.

The second flag is a default by either Italy or Spain on their national debt as such an event would have much bigger repercussions for European banks and pension funds than a Greek default. The financial numbers are much larger and the markets would probably freeze like they did in 2008. We give this Black Swan scenario a 20% probability in light of the present Eurozone crisis. The odds are now high enough for the flags to require extremely close monitoring, particularly given the risk of contagion in Europe. Remember, you can do nothing once the lightning starts except go indoors!

Hence, the best option is to make sure your financial situation remains fairly conservative, so that you can survive the storm if it hits.

The latest South African scenarios

As you will see later in the book, we now attach a 25% probability to "Failed State" and the same 25% probability to "Second Division". The red flags are rising and we must do everything to make them go down again.

Against the backdrop of the global economic scenarios, what are the possibilities for South Africa? Here are the latest scenarios for the next five years which Chantell Ilbury and I are offering our clients in South Africa.

Premier League

The International Institute for Management Development, based in Switzerland, publishes a list of 59 nations in its annual world competitiveness report. The list comes out every May and in 2012 South Africa was ranked 50 having risen from 52 last year. Before then we were in the 30s and 40s, which is where we should be as the 32nd largest economy in the world. So we are now accorded a deep discount and the reason given is that foreign investors are deterred from investing in South Africa on account of policy uncertainty here. This has not gone away as can be seen by the fact that a third of the SKA telescope project was awarded to Australia as a hedge against betting the whole shop on South Africa.

Thus, in the "Premier League" scenario we manage to get our ducks in a row and achieve much greater policy certainty. We return to the mid-30s where we rightfully belong as both overseas and local companies invest the large hoards of cash that they have been accumulating on the side-lines in our economy. They trust the rules of the game will not change.

Second Division

In the second scenario, we do not get our ducks in a row and uncertainty continues. Consequently, we slide down into the "Second Division" where the bulk of the Third World is located – poor but peaceful. Companies will still make money in South Africa as they do in many Third World economies, but for the government it is a disaster. They won't get the tax revenue that they enjoy in the "Premier League"; and they won't have the same access to foreign capital just when Eskom needs another R500 billion for its next generation of power stations – and if you believe the figure, we need another R750 billion to sustain our water supplies.

We will probably be kicked out of G20 and replaced by Nigeria which could overtake us by 2020 to become the largest economy in Africa. Nigeria already has an economy two-thirds the size of the South African economy and is currently growing by 7% p.a. versus our figure of 3% p.a. That is a differential of 4% p.a. BRICS, which we have just joined as the fifth member (alongside Brazil, Russia, India and China), will probably become BRINC!

Three flags

We have three flags for deciding whether we are going back up into the middle of the "Premier League" or sinking into the "Second Division". The first one is around inclusive leadership. We looked at nations that have done well in the "Premier League" and invariably they have had spells of inclusive leadership where the President or Prime Minister of the country has acted successfully in bringing the majority and minorities together into a cohesive team. In soccer, the most successful team as a global brand is Manchester United and it is largely due to Alex Ferguson keeping them united. Here we are in a hiatus as the top leadership in the ANC is engaged in internal politics leading up to the contest in December. Can you imagine what would happen to the performance of Manchester United in the next season if Fergie was diverting most of his attention to family squabbles?

The second flag is about pockets of excellence of which this country has many examples. If they are used to raise the performance of the nation as a whole, that is a great flag. If they are dumbed down in a bid to eliminate anything that appears elite, that would be one of the worst flags of all. We have 28 000 schools in South Africa of which 5 000 are reasonable to excellent and 23 000 are dysfunctional to shocking. If the model of the 5 000 is used to raise the performance of the 23 000, that would be excellent. If the 5 000 are dumbed down, that would be the worst flag of all in terms of our long-term competitiveness. Seeing that the main variable in a school's prospects is the principal, an academy for principals would be a step in the right direction.

The third flag is around the creation of a balanced economy: an outward economy that earns us enough foreign exchange to pay for our imports and an inward economy that creates jobs and makes a significant dent on our hideous unemployment rate. As far as the outward economy is concerned, you have to play to your strengths to win in the ultra-competitive game that now exists. There are three spaces we can dominate on the global stage:

1. Resources

Despite the decline in production of gold and diamonds, we are still number 1 in platinum, manganese and chrome and have plenty of high grade iron ore and coal. Where we can we must go downstream and add value before we export our resources.

2. Tourism

We are a relatively cheap destination, besides which we have never built on the extraordinary success of the Soccer World

Cup in 2010 (when amazingly the nation came together for one month and crime fell to an all-time low). Now is the time to offer ourselves as a real value-for-money tourist attraction.

3. Gateway into Africa

We are the largest and most advanced economy in Africa and Africa is opening for business. According to the World Bank, six of the top ten fastest growing economies in the world over the next five years are in Africa. We are the natural place for Western multinationals to kick off their campaign to access the continent's market as Walmart is doing right now.

On the inward economy, we only have one flag but it is critical: our attitude to entrepreneurs and small business. In comparing the two largest economies in the world, America and China, they cannot be more different except for one characteristic: their passion for entrepreneurs. As one young Chinese woman whose father is closely connected to the Politburo said: 'The one thing Westerners overlook about China is that Deng unleashed the entrepreneurial spirit in 1978 and that is the force which has carried us to No. 2 today. Outside of Beijing and Shanghai, there is constructive economic anarchy.' In the US, the respect that Americans have for entrepreneurs like the late Steve Jobs, the founder of Apple, is legendary.

In South Africa, the environment for entrepreneurs is extremely regulated and hostile – ranging from unreasonable labour legislation to shoddy treatment by the state, parastatals and big business as clients. Unfair price squeezing and late payment for services are real issues. Even in the report of the National Planning Commission, the focus was on infrastructure spending while the development of an entrepreneurial culture was marginalised. Our goal for 2020 should be to create one million new businesses rather than five million jobs. It is the only way to create that number of jobs. Big business has changed its employment model and now subcontracts all its non-core activities to other companies; the government has not got the money to create five million extra civil servants; and public works programmes are a temporary solution.

Hence, our odds on "Premier League" versus "Second Division" have changed from 70:30 18 months ago to 50:40 as we feel that the three flags we have selected are indicating the danger of relegation rather than the chances of promotion at the moment. We do not have inclusive leadership; we do not celebrate our pockets of excellence; and we have not changed our mind-set towards entrepreneurs. Against this, we did rise two places in the "Premier League" this year.

Failed State

Lying in the wings is a wild card scenario to which we now assign a 10% probability compared to the zero probability we had previously. It is where South Africa joins the likes of Syria, Afghanistan and Somalia as a "Failed State". Obviously, the level of violence here is nothing like it is in any of those three countries. However, we have four red flags and one tendency: if any of the flags rise or the tendency turns into reality, the odds on "Failed State" increase.

Our first red flag is nationalisation. It would be seen as a thoroughly retrogressive step by the majority of our trading partners and the question most frequently asked is where the money to pay for the mines and the banks would come from. It would appear that the ANC have come to a similar conclusion as they are now pursuing the idea of a state-owned enterprise competing against the private sector, as well as increasing royalties and other rents. This flag is therefore down at present.

The second flag is a clumsy implementation of National Health Insurance which leads to a decline in private medical care and another exodus of young talent from this country (for whom adequate health care for themselves and their families is a high priority). The Minister is in consultation with the major private sector players which again suggests this flag is down for the time being.

The third flag is a media tribunal with punitive powers which is the reason for our giving "Failed State" a 10% probability. Gagging the media is as bad as undermining the independence of the judiciary. They are both cornerstones of a modern democratic state and any weakening of either institution will remove any remaining brakes on corruption. The government has made some concessions by turning the tribunal into a public commission and putting a whistle-blower clause in the act. Nevertheless, there is other security legislation in the pipeline and the nature of a secret has not been defined.

The fourth flag is the most lethal one: land grabs which will immediately divide the nation and possibly cause a civil war. We will literally hit the wall and be off everybody's investment agenda. The whole point of identifying a red flag like this is to ask how it can be kept down. We believe that the country needs an Agridesa of all the major players in the agricultural game to negotiate a land transformation programme with a reasonable chance of success. In other words, land grabs should be pre-empted.

The tendency comes from two sessions I recently conducted with Western embassies in Pretoria. I asked them both whether they had foreseen the Arab Spring coming and they said no. I then asked whether in retrospect there were flags they missed. They said yes: abnormally high youth unemployment in all the countries affected by the Arab Spring; combined with growing alienation from the state by young people; combined with active social networks. South Africa has all three factors present and is therefore one random event away from its own version of the Arab Spring. Again, the purpose of putting this tendency on the table is to encourage anybody who listens to do all he or she can to keep the tendency from turning into reality by investigating measures to bring youth unemployment down as fast as possible.

Conclusion

If you add the 40% for "Second Division" to the 10% for "Failed State", we are now in a 50 : 50 position between the good and the bad scenarios. We therefore call this moment a second tipping point as the first tipping point occurred in the early 1990s when we could have tipped into civil war, but were saved from doing so by Codesa 1 and 2 which resulted in a new constitution and an open, democratic election. We now need a Codesa 3 or Economic Codesa in which the government, the top 100 CEOs in the private sector, the unions and other significant players in civil society participate to create an inclusive economy driven by a new generation of entrepreneurs and industrialists. The Agridesa would be a separate but linked initiative. The outcome would be a highly publicised list of targets and actions to which the participants would be held accountable jointly and severally. Implementation has always been our weak suit and this is one way of making things happen.

War games: The new normal

War games are like business games: they change dramatically in a period of five to ten years. That is why so many nations purchase inappropriate weapons and have obsolete strategies for threats which are no longer the primary ones. The use of drones is just the latest development for which countermeasures will inevitably be found to lower their effectiveness.

One of the points that Chantell Ilbury and I repeatedly make about people who are foxes is that, like the animal, they continuously scan the environment for evidence of change. On a flight to Zurich last week to do some work in Switzerland, I was casually reading *Newsweek* when I came across an article that went 'ping' in my mind – a game-changing flag had risen on the manner of war.

The article described how unmanned drones are being used to eliminate America's enemies in countries like Pakistan and Yemen. A bounty of $5m or more is offered for information that leads to the location of individuals on the intelligence agency's hit list. With the help of satellites ringing the Earth, the movement of these individuals is then precisely tracked and when a suitable opportunity arises, a Hellfire missile is dispatched from the drone to destroy the house or car accommodating the individuals targeted. Thus, the leadership of organisations dedicated to the downfall of America is being whittled down.

Very scary stuff which excludes all conventional military tactics involving mass armies, navies and manned fighters and bombers in the airforce. No battle is fought and no American has to put his life at risk. The operation is handled on a computer screen by technicians. Reportedly the targets are signed off by the US President as Commander-in-Chief in consultation with Chiefs of Staff and several lawyers. A tick against a name in a faraway country signs the death warrant.

More controversially, the *Newsweek* article also talked of "signature strikes" where it was not absolutely proven that the individual concerned had committed crimes against America. They just had the signature of being the enemy. It is one thing to profile an individual to be searched when going through Customs; but it is quite another to profile an individual for execution. Normally, you need a courtroom, a judge and a jury to hand down the death penalty in those states that allow it in the US.

What has surprised me is a subsequent article that I read elsewhere indicating that not only Republicans but the vast majority of Democrats in America are in favour of these tactics. Indeed, the information was apparently leaked in the first place to bolster support for the incumbent in the White House in the lead-up to the presidential election in December. The White House has stoutly denied this.

Wow, there are so many moral and legal questions around this approach to war. Imagine if an unmanned drone was used to take out a suspected house and its residents in Cape Town? You might say South Africa is not at war with America but neither is Yemen or Pakistan. Moreover, potential enemies in leadership positions are everywhere – even in countries like the UK. As worrying is that enemies of America may develop the same technologies and unleash a squadron of drones on the US in retaliation. Anti-ballistic missile systems will not help in such a situation.

War has just taken a different turn like it did in 1945 and with 9/11. The significance is yet to be understood.

But one thing is for sure: a satellite system allows its owner to get rid of leaders without ever engaging the followers. There is nowhere to hide from the eyes in the sky.

We need an Agridesa now

It is so easy to bury ones head in the sand on an issue as touchy as land. You have to face up to it before pressure takes the issue beyond your control.

One of the red flags which Chantell Ilbury and I have identified for South Africa turning into a failed state like Afghanistan and Somalia is land grabs. Of the four flags we have, it is probably the most lethal and emotional. The heated controversy stirred up by Pieter Mulder's remarks shows what a tinderbox issue land is. It would appear that you can use history to justify any views you wish to take on the subject from preserving the status quo to turning the whole place upside down. No issue divides citizens more deeply.

I am more interested in the future than the past and the one thing this country has shown the world is that when push comes to shove, people here can negotiate sensibly with one another. We did it in the early 1990s with Codesa 1 and 2 and we can do it again.

We need to get the major players in the agricultural sector around a table including the commercial farmers, the emerging farmers, AgriSA and other representative bodies, government and Land Bank delegates, union officials, rural community members and subsistence farmers and anyone else who is important in determining the outcome of the game.

I would suggest a 10-point agenda for this Agridesa or whatever you would like to call it. It is the one Chantell and I use whenever we facilitate strategy sessions for companies and other organisations. We have, however, found that the model works just as well when you bring disparate players with conflicting interests together to debate the best way they can co-operate with one another to produce a mutually acceptable result.

Obviously, there has to be give and take and nobody can pursue their own end-game to the exclusion of everyone else. The objective is to maintain a viable game where no one emerges as an outright winner or loser, the alternative being the destruction of the entire game with abnormal losses for every party to it.

The agenda is as follows.

1. Context

In order to consider what is possible in taking the game to a higher level, one must understand how the game has changed over the past 10 to 20 years. Agriculture is totally different now to what it was in the 1990s. Food on this planet is becoming scarce and, as a friend of mine said, there is no planet B. Indeed, environmental degradation is reducing the productive potential of our one and only planet. On the other hand, population growth is ensuring rising demand for food products and hence higher prices. Why else do you think the Chinese are buying fertile land in Australia, Indonesia and Africa? Under context, one must also come closer to home and examine why the programme for transforming land ownership in this country has so far been slow and yielded so few successes.

2. Scope

Every playing field has boundaries and it is important to determine them. In this case, there has to be a fairly precise definition of the problem that has to be resolved. Are we talking about physical land which has to be transferred from white to black hands or are we talking about dividing up farming businesses on a more equitable basis?

There is a big difference between the two as the one calls for exchange of title between individuals while the other calls for the kind of solution that has already taken place in manufacturing and mining, namely changing the ratio of equity ownership. What about vacant land and land owned by the state? Does scope only cover farm land or does it extend to land used for other activities like game reserves? To arrive at acceptable answers, you have to understand exactly what the question is and focus on it, disregarding all other issues.

3. Players

This part of the conversation follows logically from the previous one. Now that we have established the playing field and its boundaries, who are the key players on the field and how are they going to add value in terms of producing a constructive result to the game? How are the large agri-businesses going to share their expertise to give emerging farmers a greater chance of success? Who are the ideal sources of capital to finance the deals that need to be done?

4. Rules

What should the rules of the game be to ensure that the transformation process is orderly and maintains security of food supplies? This is a sensitive area as one of the principles that has to be debated is the willing-buyer/willing-seller one. Equally what rules will apply to foreign ownership?

5. Key uncertainties

What are the surprises that one should have on the radar screen so that they do not deflect the game from a positive outcome? How does one prepare for them or mitigate their impact? No game is ever smooth and one must develop the ability to adapt one's strategy when necessary. For me, one of the big uncertainties is how the global and South African economies will perform during the period allocated to resolving this issue. It is much tougher changing things during economic hard times.

6. Scenario gameboard

At this stage one should construct a gameboard showing good and bad outcomes and ask where South African agriculture is on the board at the moment. The two axes should represent the two main concerns of the players and the scenario for each quadrant should have an appropriate title. Here is my best shot as an illustration:

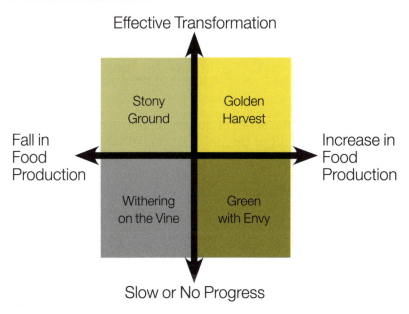

Going clockwise from bottom right, "Green with Envy" is a scenario of increasing hostility to existing commercial farmers as they grow their businesses without any improvement in owner representivity. It remains a white preserve.

"Withering on the Vine" is where food production falls domestically as existing farmers are loath to re-invest in their farms as a result of all the uncertainty surrounding land ownership. South Africa has to pay through the nose for food imports.

"Stony Ground" likewise is where there is a fall in local food production because the seeds of transformation have not been properly sown. Many emerging farmers fail through lack of support.

"Golden Harvest" is where true representivity is achieved among farm owners, but at the same time improvements in productivity are elicited because the environment for investment has stabilised. Everybody understands the rules and they don't change. Successful black commercial farmers co-operate and vie with their white counterparts. So where is the South African farming industry now and where is it heading? How can we make it go in the right direction?

7. SWOT

This is a transitional series of questions before the agenda gets to the business end of the negotiations of what to do. What are the strengths and weaknesses of South African agriculture at the moment and what are the opportunities and threats posed by the changes in the international food game? In other words, where do we stand internationally and what strategies can we pursue to raise our attractiveness in the eyes of local and foreign customers in the food business?

8. Options

What are the available options within the control of the parties around the table to move South African agriculture towards the "Golden Harvest" scenario? What are the strategic options in setting a new direction and what are the tactical options to improve the chances of getting there?

9. Decisions

Who around the table is going to do what by when in order to get the show on the road? A hard timetable with hard targets has to be agreed at this stage of the Agridesa proceedings. It will not be possible to come up with a complete list of actions into the long-term future and many of the initial decisions will be around examining the optimum way of executing the options at the top of the list of priorities. The second phase will be actual implementation.

10. The meaning of winning

What are the measurable outcomes that the parties would like to achieve in the next five years to get the feeling that they are winning the game? Two years is too short, ten years is too long. The agreed measurable outcomes can constitute a score-card against which progress can be measured. Additional items can be added to the list at any time.

It would be first prize for the government to be the lead actor in arranging an Agridesa. If they are unwilling to do so, a neutral body like the South African Institute of Race Relations could be the organiser. Remember failure to act urgently on this issue will result in what Anne Robinson says to the loser each night on *The Weakest Link*: "You leave with nothing."

Peace or war: It's your call

This article really backs up the previous one in terms of the urgency for a constructive solution to land reform.

With the report on the News24 website that ANCYL's Deputy President, Ronald Lamola, stated that an act as forceful as war was needed to bring the land back to Africans, I would like to repeat the comment I made in a previous article on the latest South African scenarios:

'The fourth flag [for a "Failed State" scenario] is the most lethal one: land grabs which will immediately divide the nation and possibly cause a civil war. We will literally hit the wall and be off everybody's investment agenda. The whole point of identifying a red flag like this is to ask how it can be kept down. We [Chantell Ilbury and I] believe that the country needs an Agridesa of all the major players in the agricultural game to negotiate a land transformation programme with a reasonable chance of success. In other words, land grabs should be pre-empted.'

What more can we say as futurists desperately wanting our country to stay in the "Premier League" of nations and maintain its status as the leading and most advanced economy in Africa? We currently assign a 10% probability to the "Failed State" scenario which is up from the zero probability we were giving it 18 months ago. Quite a few commentators and companies attach a much higher probability, with the latter actively seeking ways of extending their geographical footprint into other African countries where they have a greater trust in a peaceful future. I am not kidding when I say that the CEOs doing this are probably giving 50:50 odds to a future of peace or war in South Africa.

In other words, the fear is that we turn into an old version of Liberia and Sierra Leone, where child soldiers with newly acquired AK47s are driven around on Toyota pick-ups and atrocities become a daily occurrence. The infrastructure of the country is completely degraded, the economy goes into a precipitous dive and the only issues are starvation and lack of medical facilities to treat the dying and wounded. The critical variable then becomes whether the war is purely a black-versus-white affair or whether it descends into ethnic strife with shifting allegiances and all the chaos that entails.

We have to face up to one fact. While we have a free and fair political system, we do not have a free and fair economy. Citizens of South Africa certainly have political freedom, but not economic freedom. The economy is far too centralised and lop-sided to be anything like one which can be called inclusive. For all those critics who talk about an absence of work ethic among the citizenry, I would totally disagree. Entrepreneurs in South Africa are in chains because of their shoddy treatment by government, parastatals and big business who seem to have formed an unholy alliance to keep the economy in as few hands as possible. The unions don't help by pursuing a very narrow definition of decent work which means either unionised employment or no employment at all. The informal sector, instead of being supported, is frowned upon and ignored.

So I will end with the conclusion Chantell Ilbury and I put forward in the article:

"We therefore call this moment a second tipping point as the first tipping point occurred in the early 1990s when we could have tipped into civil war, but were saved from doing so by Codesa 1 and 2 which resulted in a new constitution and an open, democratic election. We now need a Codesa 3 or Economic Codesa in which the government, the top 100 CEOs in the private sector, the unions and other significant players in civil society participate to create an inclusive economy driven by a new generation of entrepreneurs and industrialists."

The disappearing art of handwriting

I have heard that as a species our thumbs are growing in length as a result of adapting to the need to type text messages!

There I was on the side of the aisle at the extreme back of the aircraft handwriting a column for News24. It was the two-hour flight from Cape Town to Johannesburg in the late morning and you have plenty of time to read or write.

On the other side of the aisle was a young woman on her way to a friend's wedding, fretting that she had left her husband in charge of the children for the whole weekend. This I ascertained when I glanced across to see what she was doing to occupy herself during the flight. She had her laptop computer open and was playing the keys like a classical pianist. Her speed made me envious as I am still part of the two-finger brigade that has to search for a specific letter or punctuation mark.

In a similar way, she was checking what I was doing and smiled. 'That is the difference between the generations,' she said. 'You are communicating with pen and paper and I am communicating with printed text on the screen.' We then had a fascinating conversation around how often she used handwriting to get her message across. It turned out to be making lists, filling out forms and signing her name. All personal stuff was handled by SMS or e-mail. Again I am in awe of the two-thumb technique involved in dashing off an SMS, whereas I hold the phone in one hand and prod it with the other.

She said her children were computer-savvy at the ages of five and six and took their mobile phones everywhere, even to school. But, and this is the whole point of the chapter, she grimaced as she added: 'They can hardly write their names, let alone an essay or letter.' It is true: the younger generation are beginning to lose the ability to write with their hands as they do it much more infrequently than I used to do it when I was their age. It is like sport. You have to practise to be any good at it.

As I write this chapter, I have in front of me a letter written by my late mother in the 1980s thanking me for a wonderful holiday she and my father had in South Africa. She ends it with the words: 'God speed, all the luck in the world, and you are and always will be our most dear son.' Somehow, in a handwritten form, these words are so much more beautiful than in a printed e-mail which I might well have deleted anyway. Also, they are part of my mother which nothing on a computer can really be. Handwriting is the extension of the spirit through the movement of the hand. Her style is unique in contrast to the printed word which is always the same.

There. I wrote this chapter without making one mistake.

If I was young, gifted and black

At some stage, the voices of the young black citizens of this country will be heard and people will be surprised by the message.

If I was young, gifted and black I would have this to say after attending an ANC policy meeting:

What is it about you guys that makes you cloak everything in dead white Russian speak? I managed to wade through 'The Second Transition' on the internet and the language used reminded me of stuff Lenin or Stalin would have used. Calling these ideas progressive is like me saying to my friends that Elvis Presley is the coolest musician ever whilst humming 'Teddy Bear' in my blue suede shoes.

Get real. This is 2013 not 1917 and we are in Africa, not the Soviet Union. Even the Russians have moved on now that they realise that most of their socialist 'yada yada' was used to cover up their leaders putting fingers in the cookie jar. I want an African solution to our problems not a discredited one from the northern hemisphere. After all, you are the ANC with the emphasis on the word 'A'.

Talking of solutions, what would I have wanted out of your bash last week (and my answers are not going to cost you R45m)? Firstly, as a young person, I want a better education system for which you are entirely responsible. I do not want handouts, I want to gain the knowledge and skills which will allow me to be self-sufficient and choose whatever career I wish bearing in mind my own strengths and weaknesses. I may even want to become an entrepreneur and start my own business. In other words, I don't want to be an employee of yours or anybody else's. I will do my own thing and maybe have other employees working for me. Why should you deny me the opportunity by denying me a decent education? The last thing I am going to do is spend my life grovelling in front of politicians so that I can stay alive. I want it my way, not yours.

I would have liked the delegation from each province to have pledged that they would improve a specific number of schools every year in their domain. They would be held to the targets that they set. Conferences without measurable outcomes are useless exercises in hot air. Get your own house in order before offering opinions on what others should do in theirs.

Secondly, I would have hoped for a radical shift towards deconcentrating our economy. All you offered was further concentration in state hands. What makes you think that you are better at spotting commercial opportunities and making money out of them when you have never personally started a business in your life? Look at your current record. We need much greater economic democracy where entrepreneurs – the guys who really can spot an opportunity and turn it into a commercial reality – are given a proper shot at success.

Why don't you consider a basic investment grant as opposed to a basic income grant? Entrepreneurs don't like borrowing money at any interest rate given the chance of failure. They need equity finance and you can provide it.

Thirdly, and lastly, please get your act together. Can you imagine how the pupils in a school would feel if the teachers spent their time away from the classroom having a row over who the principal should be in the common room? They would feel utterly let down. You guys must stop having leadership contests and settle down to governing this country in a way that gives young people like me hope that there is a future here.

A National Leadership Academy

Nick Binedell's idea is a great one and should be part of the National Development Plan.

I was chatting to Nick Binedell yesterday at the Gordon Institute of Business Science in Johannesburg. He is the Director of this business school and is widely acknowledged for his role of turning the institution into one of the leading centres of business education in Africa. He agrees with me that the time has come for an Economic Codesa, but worries that there is not yet the same sense of crisis that drove the principal parties into a Political Codesa in the early 1990s.

He suggested that one of the items on the agenda should be the establishment of a National Leadership Academy to train leaders at all three levels of government – national, provincial and municipal. I totally agree with him because, in the words of the late Frederick van Zyl Slabbert, we suffer from a crisis of implementation. We have lots of ideas, talk, workshops, plans and summits, but we do not have a good conversion rate of turning all the things we agree should be done into action.

Apart from that, an essential part of modern leadership is good corporate governance whether you are in the public or private sector. In this regard, the public judges the leaders by their deeds and not by their words. Equally, given the hard economic times, a good nose for what is cost-effective and what is mere squandering of funds is an important characteristic of the head of any organisation.

Personally, I do not feel there is much difference between being the CEO of a major company and being the CEO of a country, a province or town. You have to understand the game you are in; you have to inspire your followers to go the extra mile; you have to be good at persuading others to your point of view; you need to be intelligent about strategy and tactics; you should be smart about encouraging innovation among your staff; you have to be consistent and fair; and above all you must hold your immediate team accountable for their actions and make sure the principle of accountability is driven down to the lowest level of the organisation.

Right now, one of the flags that Chantell Ilbury and I feel is critical in judging whether South Africa stays in the "Premier League" of nations is inclusive leadership. You need the majority and minority to have that universal feeling of being part of the same team. In sports like rugby, soccer and cricket, you only win trophies with a united side and the same absolutely applies to countries. Hence, class and racial divisions are the kiss of death when they seriously disrupt the national spirit. A good leader tolerates diversity but never allows diversity to descend into outright division.

All these characteristics and much more could be taught at a National Leadership Academy. As Nick rightly says, companies obsess about their competitors and how the quality of their internal strategy and marketing can have a positive or negative impact on their market capitalisation. What they fail to understand is that the success or failure of the country in which they operate can have a far bigger impact on their net worth.

Thus, it is a no-brainer if we are to have a social compact between government and business as a result of an Economic Codesa that one of the elements should be a leadership academy catering for the special qualities necessary to be a leader in the South African context. Perhaps we will then get things done which leads to a better life for all while vanquishing the triple-headed monster of poverty, inequality and unemployment.

Madiba and Alex: Two inclusive leaders

Turning a diverse group of individuals into a coherent team is one of the most important tasks of a leader.

Happy birthday, Madiba! You have now, in 2012, outlasted my mother by nearly three years. I always knew her age because you turned it three months before she did. Like my mother made me feel special all my life, you made me feel very special when I visited you in prison in January 1990 just before your release.

I say all this because the real art of leadership is to make people feel wanted and special and part of a team to which they can make a contribution for its success. You did that very well in your brief five years at the helm. We were a nation setting off on a path, full of hope and fear but united.

Which brings me to Alex Ferguson who is visiting this country at the moment with the team he manages, Manchester United. Why do you think that he has won more trophies than any other manager in the history of the game of soccer? Simple. He employs the same principles as Madiba in turning a bunch of diverse individuals into a coherent team. Whenever one of his stars wants to walk out to another club, he calls him in and irons out the problems and re-invigorates his commitment to the club.

Alex is now in his 70s just as you were when you took over the reins of this country. It shows that leaders can go on being leaders until they die. There is no retirement age! A source of inspiration is always a source of inspiration.

Moreover, nations are like soccer teams. They compete on the world stage and those that demonstrate hard work, have

a belief in themselves and constantly exercise a spirit of innovation are the ones that win the game. They score the goals
they set themselves – in our case a better life for all.

So, may you both continue to have rich and productive lives
making your followers feel that they are walking alongside
you, making them feel included in the grand enterprise to
which you have dedicated your entire existence. You have
shown that winning the game together is not the only thing.
It is everything.

Parallel economic universes

Thabo Mbeki's point about South Africa being a country of two economies was right on the button. We have to marry the two.

1. Introduction and definition of U1/U2

Sadly, South Africa has two economic universes which are light years away from one another. The first universe is the formal part of the economy which for the purpose of this chapter I shall call U1. It is the one inhabited by government, large to medium-sized businesses, the trade unions and all the employees involved in the public and formal private sector. U1 transactions can be large as in new power stations or small as in purchases at a retail chain. The growth of the U1 economy relies on an increase in size and frequency of those transactions.

The second universe, or U2 economy, is what we normally refer to as the informal sector. It is entirely populated by small to micro business, experienced and new entrepreneurs alike, social entrepreneurs who have opened up NGOs and of course all those who work for them where they have employees. Transactions in the U2 space tend to be small unless an entrepreneur strikes it lucky. Rather, it is the number of transactions and velocity of circulation of relatively small amounts of money that determine the viability of the U2 economy.

2. International examples of U1/U2 economies

America has always been a hybrid U1/U2 economy on account of the importance placed on the role of entrepreneurship there. The culture of individualism has also meant that many Americans want to do their own thing in the U2 economy in preference to working for someone in the U1 economy. Britain, in the early stages of the Industrial Revolution, was a U2 economy, but over time it has evolved into a fairly uncompetitive U1 economy because of socialist policies and the barriers created by the class system. The gaping holes left by the disappearance of such industries as coal mining, steel and ship-building have never really been filled by new U2 entrants in the regions affected.

Japan and Germany are interesting. Having been flattened in the Second World War, neither of them suffered from the dominance of a U1 economy in the aftermath. Their resurrection was due to a balanced resurgence of both their U1 and U2 economies working in conjunction with one another. That relationship propelled Japan into one of the top three global economies and Germany to be the champion of present-day Europe. The dismal failure of many of the other European nations shows the disconnect between the U1 and U2 components of their economies.

Turning to the New World, India has basically been a U2 economy since its independence. It was shackled by an overprotective bureaucracy for a long time but has more recently been liberated. Voila, the annual economic growth rate of India soared from 2% to 8% and now large family businesses are making their presence felt in U1 economies worldwide. Brazil and Chile are notable exponents of granting greater status to their U2 brethren while guarding their U1 mining industries.

In Africa, the U2 revolution is occurring in virtually every sub-Saharan economy other than South Africa. The most powerful example of a U2 economy is Nigeria with Lagos being tipped to take over from Johannesburg as Africa's leading city. The Nigerian film industry which is still very much in the U2 stage has recently ascended to number 2 in the world behind India – the ranking is Bollywood, Nollywood, then Hollywood! The sheer entrepreneurial frenzy of the streets of

Lagos is in direct contrast to the empty streets in Sandton other than people crossing the road to catch the Gautrain. Lagos currently resembles Hong Kong or Bangkok in its display of U2 businesses in every nook and cranny around town.

Which brings us to the Far East. The success of the Asian Tigers like South Korea, Singapore, Malaysia and Vietnam bears testament to the strength of their U2 economies and the fact that this lays the foundation for a growing U1 presence in industries like cars, computers and smartphones. The showcase of them all is China. As one Chinese woman whose father is closely connected to the Politiburo said to me the other day: 'Westerners completely miss the principal driving force behind China shooting up 98 places in 33 years to become the second largest economy in the world. It is not foreign investment or state-owned enterprise though both played their part. The real reason was that Deng unleashed the entrepreneurial spirit of our country in 1978 and constructive economic anarchy has prevailed ever since.' In South Africa, every town has its U2 China shop and the latest figure for Chinese-owned small clothing businesses across all provinces is 10 000. Elsewhere in Africa, the pattern is being repeated.

3. The history of U1/U2 in South Africa

When all those 19th century diggers were around in Kimberley and Johannesburg prospecting for and extracting diamonds and gold, South Africa was a U2 economy. With the consolidation of the mining industry and the formation of large state-owned corporations, we rapidly turned into a highly centralised U1 economy. Apartheid completely stunted the growth of the U2 economy as black entrepreneurs were severely restricted in the geographical areas in which they could do business.

After 1994, over-regulation and sheer ignorance of the workings of a U2 economy have substituted for apartheid in destroying any potential for growth. At the recent ANC policy conference in Midrand, nationalisation dominated the debate which is all about changing the ownership of the U1 economy. Apparently, little if nothing was said about fostering the growth of enterprise in the U2 sector. The SACP has never given the idea of small worker co-operatives the passion it deserves as a key component of the U2 economy. The National Planning Commission document is totally U1-oriented with its recommendation of boosting infrastructural projects. Entrepreneurship was hardly given a mention which is not surprising as nobody on the NPC has experienced the U2 world.

Black economic empowerment has concentrated solely on changing ownership and management structures in the U1 universe. Even when BEE was converted to broad-based empowerment, it was still restricted to U1. Generally speaking, big business has utter contempt for the parallel universe of U2 and in particular uses its authorised vendor programmes as an excuse to pay the defenceless U2 suppliers and service providers months after the goods or services have been provided. Big business also gouges unreasonable discounts out of smaller enterprises using its superior negotiating clout.

The only company I know of which actively incorporates U2 players in its supply chain is Anglo American through its Zimele programme. The banks steer clear of the U2 sector given that transaction costs overshadow the interest payable on micro loans and they have no way of evaluating the risks. I would bet you that not a single bank economist could tell you what the growth rate of the Sowetan economy was last year or which township economy in South Africa performed best.

Lastly, the financial media in this country is totally focused on the U1 economy whether we are talking about newspapers, the internet, TV or radio. It is as if the U2 economy does not exist. But then they would not get the readership, viewership or listenership if they devoted too much time to the U2 champions. The exception is 702 with its Lead SA initiative.

Conclusion

So there you have it. We are a totally U1-based economy even though many of the great businesses in this country began their life as U2 gambles. If we are to meet the target of creating five million jobs by 2020, it will largely be as a result of creating one million new businesses in the U2 economy. We must do everything to find out more about it and then nurture the animal spirits – as Keynes would say – which make entrepreneurs bet their life and their money on new start-ups.

Steve Biko would agree with every word in this column because he believed that life was about people doing it for themselves. That is real empowerment and China, India, Brazil and Nigeria are great examples to follow in terms of a U2 revolution here.

Let's lease Cape Town Stadium to the U2 economy

I thought I would follow up my last column with a practical example. I got a lot of flack from Capetonians in comments on News24 for this suggestion. Meanwhile, the stadium site is sitting there virtually unused, with rate-payers forking out for its upkeep.

In the previous article I explained the difference between the visible U1 formal economy in South Africa and the invisible U2 informal economy. I stressed that if the country wants to create five million jobs by 2020, most of them will be as a result of allowing entrepreneurs to establish one million new U2 businesses.

The DA has now issued its manifesto stressing the importance of introducing accountability in education and liberating the environment for small business. That could lead South Africa to a level of economic growth – 8% per annum – enjoyed by many other African countries. Hurray for the DA putting a stake in the ground which supports my belief of giving young people entrepreneurial skills and the freedom to do their own thing.

However, I want to test the commitment of the DA to the U2 economy. I want them to do something unusual, something which is in their power to do and something which shifts the national mindset away from the U1 universe and who should own what in it. I want the debate to move on from nationalisation to how we can decentralise and democratise the economy which is far too over-centralised as a consequence of mining being the flywheel for most of the last century. Now is the time to change step and promote other sectors which are conducive to the growth of small enterprise – with the chance that some of these players will blossom and lay the foundations for the nation to become world class in new and unexpected markets.

For me, a flagship event would be to turn the Cape Town World Cup soccer stadium into a permanent market bazaar and hub for small business. At the moment, its future is still uncertain and I have even heard rumours that it could be demolished because of the high maintenance costs. I know that it is used for the odd soccer match and pop concert and there were moves to try and make it the Stormers' new home. However, it would be much more in the interests of the community to do what I am suggesting and start the process of integrating the U1 and U2 economies in the Western Cape.

Obviously, the architecture of the stadium would have to be modified in order to accommodate vendors and stalls. It would mean removing all the seats and creating levels so that the place becomes a gigantic open-air department store with different floors. The pitch could be used too as a fairground for recreational activities or serve as additional shopping space. The top tiers, with their superb all-round views of Cape Town and Table Mountain, could be reserved for coffee shops and maybe even the odd bistro.

Look, it's just an idea and specialists in redesigning large structures may rule it out on the grounds of cost or physical impossibility. Rents would have to be reasonable. I just think it is a perfect opportunity for the DA to send out a radical message about the U2 economy. The latter is no longer a sideshow but the backbone of future enterprise in this country. They could even change the name to Greenmarket Stadium and link it to the square in central Cape Town. Maybe the slogan for both should be: U2 (you too) can make a contribution to the revolution.

Do Europeans exist?

The anxiety over the possible break-up of the Eurozone appears to have subsided, but nationalist movements are making their presence felt in many member countries. The experiment is still at an early stage, given the long stretch of history.

Recently, I went to Switzerland to address a meeting mainly composed of bankers most of whom worked in European countries. I was asked to present the latest global economic scenarios with particular reference to the future of the Eurozone. One of the scenarios, to which I attach a 20% probability, is a default by Italy or Spain triggering another round of financial panic similar to what occurred in 2008. The scenario is called "Forked Lightning" and once the lightning starts, there is not much you can do about it other than to go inside and wait for the lightning to stop.

One of the consequences is a possible break-up of the Euro with the countries going back to their original currencies. Interestingly, one of the members of the audience raised the notion that the first country to exit would not be Greece but Germany leaving the rest to fend for themselves. I thought this was unlikely as Germany's exports are doing very well as a result of the cheap Euro.

However, it was at the dinner table that evening that the most fascinating conversation took place. The question was raised as to whether a species called Europeans really exists. You have Germans, French, Spanish, Italians, Poles, and Hungarians but each have a different history, culture and language. They have different perceptions about one another not all of which are favourable. The idea that Brussels could turn this diverse collection of nations into a homogeneous group appeared quite far-fetched.

The example of the USA was raised where it is a reality that you have Americans. As one person at the table pointed out, California is probably as broke as Greece and, if not California, one of the other smaller American states. Yet this is covered up by the fact that most people look at America as a whole when it comes to judging the future of their economy. They do not drill down to individual states. Moreover, Americans have a common history even if Spanish is rivalling English as a dominant language in parts of the country. The citizens of America feel American despite many being recent immigrants. They put their hands on their chest when shown the stars and stripes. Their loyalty is assured.

By contrast, very few citizens of the individual countries that make up Europe feel European. No sense of common patriotism exists and when the going gets tough - as it is doing now – the average person in the street reverts to his or her basic roots. The opportunity for co-operation across borders diminishes in a "Hard Times" scenario. Accordingly, your average German believes that no more money should be lent to Greece and certainly Germany's credit rating should not be tainted by the much lower rating of its southern neighbours. On the other hand, your average Greek, Italian or Spaniard feels that it is monstrously unfair that he or she has to take the full knock of increasingly severe austerity measures in order to save the Euro. Why not have ones own currency which can be devalued to stimulate exports and tourism?

Another point made in the discussion during the main course was that America has one head – President Obama – to whom all state governors are technically subservient. There is no way Angela Merkel is going to answer to the head of the European Commission like a state governor. Nor is any other head of state in Europe for that matter. So the proposition of getting a sufficient level of co-operation among members of the European Union to achieve fiscal and banking union to prop up monetary union may be imaginary.

I came away from the whole conversation wondering if the Euro was simply a bridge too far and an excuse for Brussels to have an enormously expensive bureaucracy. The whole European project should have been restricted to having a common market with nations trading in their own currencies. Some would say that is water under the bridge, but the tide can turn and water can flow in the opposite direction. Which brings me to my last point. I find it staggering that no major financial institution that I know of, no prominent economist that specialises in currencies and no futuristic think-tank in London or elsewhere has publicly played Euro break-up scenarios. What actually happens to holders of Euros? Do citizens get their own currency while foreigners outside Europe get a basket of currencies? How much will they lose?

Please tell me as I am now getting anxious. The situation is very messy and changes day by day. Markets rise, markets fall as fear comes and goes. It is forever thus but a little enlightenment would go a long way.

My eight Olympic lessons

I just hope that we provide our star athletes with the kind of support which will lead to another cluster of gold, silver and bronze medals at the next Olympic Games. Raising the money to finance their participation in overseas competitions during the interim period is vital for success.

After the final episode of the games, which I watched like a series most nights on television, I wondered how the spectacle struck me apart from its entertainment value?

I learned eight important things from the experience:

1 **No affirmative action is required provided the training is good.** The Jamaicans beat the Americans in the one area that Americans have always excelled – sprint events. There are two obvious reasons for this: Jamaicans now have training programmes equivalent in quality to Americans and right now they are ahead of Americans on natural talent. However, the same can be said across most other events whether we are talking archery, fencing or men's javelin. Unusual nations are winning them. My point has been reinforced that if you want to be a winning nation, it comes down to education, education and education. That is why teaching is one of the most highly paid professions in Singapore. But then teachers there are held accountable for results just like coaches are in athletics.

2 **The rules of each sport apply equally to everybody participating.** No exceptions are allowed on the grounds of fame, wealth, gender or age. Moreover, retribution is swift if the rules are broken. For example, when a participant

jumps the gun at the start of a running or swimming event, he or she is now ruled out of the competition unless some reasonable cause can be established. The consequence is that, unlike in the past, there are very few false starts disrupting proceedings. The Olympics work because of law and order. The same applies to countries.

3 **The human race is a competitive species.** If you want to win, you have to do your homework, prepare yourself over many years of toil, work out your strategy with due regard for the characteristics of your rivals and perform on the actual day. What applies in sport applies to any other career. In addition, should you be part of a team, you have to learn to co-operate with others and even on occasion sacrifice your own interests of achieving individual excellence to the interests of the team in order to win the game. Cycling is a very good illustration of this principle in action in the team events. Most organised human activity is collective, not individual, and requires the same degree of unselfishness.

4 **We win gold in many different fields.** The variation of sports on display at the Olympics is dazzling. It features humans in all shapes and sizes from the giants in weightlifting with whom you would not mess around if they caught your eye in the street to the young, fragile ballerinas involved in gymnastics. It would suggest that, in real life, a society should offer its citizens as wide a range of legal pursuits as it is possible to do because a champion will be found in even the most esoteric niche. Diversity of calling is the essence of living.

5 **There are winners and losers, but sometimes losers are winners.** In this politically correct age, everybody expects equal treatment and indeed you are scarcely permitted to differentiate individuals on performance, rewarding some with bonuses and others not. Thank heavens in the Olym-

pics this outlook does not apply. To be an Olympian is an honour, but to be a medallist is special and certainly not something to be sneered at because it too is elite. Yet, non-medallists in a particular event can be winners for a host of other reasons, like beating your personal best, accepting defeat gracefully or overcoming a major handicap.

6 **Words mean nothing in the Olympic Games, only deeds on the field.** Think of how many times you have heard the phrase on television that the problem is being attended to or appropriate steps are underway – and then nothing happens! In sport, medals are not rewarded for rhetoric. Furthermore, when world records are broken, it is a sobering thought that you are witnessing a deed that has never happened before in the history of mankind.

7 **Youth is really beautiful and ogling is perfectly okay.** My pick of the female athletes was Anna Chicherova, the Russian high jump medallist. The way she eyed the bar made me feel weak at the knees. A close second was Carli Lloyd who was in the winning US soccer team and scored both goals in the final. It was not so much her looks as the quality of her second goal which proved she could bend it just like David Beckham. Magnificent even if I watched it on the screen thousands of miles away.

8 **National flags count as much as the universal message of the Olympic symbol.** Over 200 countries were represented at the games, so there were a lot of flags on display and a lot of national anthems. Somehow, the Olympics manage to bring out the best in us by kindling the national spirit in a very positive way while sending out the signal that we all live in one world. Sport is better than war and one can celebrate the victory of another country particularly when the individual is as charismatic as Usain Bolt. Nevertheless, the biggest kick comes from

watching ones own athletes picking up the medals. So congratulations to Cameron, Chad, our four-man rowing crew of Sizwe, Matthew, John and James, Caster and Bridgette. You did us proud and made us forget about our divisions back home for just a short moment in time. Thanks to all the members of Team South Africa for the joy you gave us and laying the foundation for 2016 in Rio.

Marikana: A major red flag overseas and at home

Marikana was a terrible tragedy. One hopes the Commission of Enquiry will get to the bottom of the causes and provide effective recommendations to ensure no repetition. For me, the one new feature is the heavy amount of debt the average miner takes on, the repayment of which is automatically deducted from the monthly payroll. That can significantly add to the tension and has to be carefully managed so that the amount does not get out of hand.

One of the points that Chantell Ilbury and I have been making for the last few years is that we live in an ultra-competitive world; and, if we want a better life for all, we have to stay in the "Premier League" of nations. Relegation to the "Second Division" or, worse still, descending into a "Failed State" kills any chance of achieving the levels of economic growth (6 to 8% p.a.) necessary for a universal upliftment in South African living standards.

Alas, no matter what words of comfort are offered by our government ministers when being interviewed by an international news agency, Marikana has done enormous damage to our brand of being a thoroughly modern democracy at the tip of Africa – indeed an exceptional model for the rest of Africa to follow. Just for starters, if this incident happened in America, Britain, Europe, Canada, Japan or Australia, the government would have immediately resigned and fresh elections would have been called.

The closest example I can think of in magnitude to this tragedy occurred on 30 January 1972 in the Bogside area of

Derry, Northern Ireland when 26 unarmed civil-rights protesters and bystanders were shot by soldiers of the British Army. It became known as Bloody Sunday. Thirteen died immediately and one succumbed to his injuries four and a half months later. Northern Ireland was a highly troubled region at the time.

It will take a huge amount of effort to restore our image of being a decent, moral society and an attractive investment destination. Rather than trying to predict the findings of the commission of inquiry into the tragic incident itself, I would prefer to give my list of actions to begin the path of recovery in the eyes of the world as well as of our own citizens.

1 **Implement employee share ownership programmes across all mines.** Having been in the mining industry all my life, I am very much aware that we should be doing all we can to improve the conditions of the miners at the face. The problem with tripling wages is that it could lead to the closure of shafts or even whole mines. It would be much better to do what Kumba has done and bring in the miners as part owners. That means they will do well in good times for the mining industry but are less likely to be retrenched in hard times. For me, anyway, it makes much more sense for the ownership of the mines to be extended to the workers rather than for the mines to be nationalised.

2 **Stop militarising the police.** The game of an army is to use maximum force to defeat the enemy. The game of the police is to impose law and order using minimum force. They are totally different games requiring completely different strategies and tactics. They should never be combined as this only increases the odds of a disaster like Marikana.

3 **Cease cadre deployment.** The flag of violence has always

been our principal flag for assigning a probability to our "Failed State" scenario. Criminal violence has been around for a long time but now you can add public violence caused by frustrations over lack of service delivery. The only way the latter is going to improve is to hire individuals and companies with proven track records to do the job. So much could be done for so much less money if the normal management principles that are part and parcel of running any competitive world-class business in the private sector are adhered to by the players in the public sector.

4 **Achieve a new economic accord.** For over a year now, I have been proposing the idea of an Economic Codesa to try and align our U1 economy of big business, the unions and government with the U2 economy of entrepreneurs and small business. At the moment, we have parallel economic universes with no linkages between the two and little if no hope for the inhabitants of the U2 economy. It will require a private-public partnership of note to create the possibility of integrating the two universes and thereby ushering in a new era of economic democracy and freedom. It has to start with a big bang accord to which all parties commit.

When something like Marikana happens, you want to make sure that the tragedy of it all compels people to take a different and better path to the one they were on prior to the event. Let's change step while the emotions are still raw so that nobody in the entire saga died in vain. You cannot turn back the clock, but you can create a better future.

How the world turns

How swift is the zero-to-hero-to-zero cycle! Celebrity is ephemeral.

I was ensconced in a repeat of *Notting Hill* the other night on DSTV. I like the movie because I was brought up halfway between Notting Hill Gate and Kensington and used to go and buy comics like Beano and Dandy and sweets called gobstoppers from a newsagent in Notting Hill. Interestingly, whereas Kensington has always been full of London toffs, Notting Hill has been more alternative and cosmopolitan.

Back to the movie. There is a stunning moment when Hugh Grant who plays the owner of a bookshop in Notting Hill invites Julia Roberts who plays an American film star around for dinner to meet his friends and family. One of his friends is Bernie, a bumbling stockbroker, who casually asks Julia Roberts what her occupation is. She replies that she is an actress and he commiserates about the poor pay in the theatre world as he has not recognised her. Then he asks her how much she earned for her last part. She replies: '15 million dollars.' That is when the penny drops that he is in the presence of a superstar and he realises what a fool he has made of himself. His face is a picture of crimson.

Later, they all do a very British thing at the dinner table and discuss who should be awarded the prize for being the biggest failure. Each person argues vehemently that he or she should get the prize. Anyway, this time I recognised the stockbroker. It was none other than a younger version of Hugh Bonneville who now plays the Earl of Grantham in the hit series *Downton Abbey*. It has become the most nominated non-American programme in Primetime Emmy history by attracting 27 nominations in its first two series. Recently, Bonneville was recognised by an elderly female fan in a vegetable market in Los Angeles who immediately had to be given assistance for hyperventilation. She eventually calmed down.

How the world turns! We really have not heard anything spectacular about Roberts and Grant for a long time. She has made a couple of movies in the past two years which have not drawn much critical acclaim and he has been named as one of the victims of the phone hacking scandal in the UK. So we could reverse the roles in another movie called *Notting Hill 2*. Julia Roberts plays the wife of Hugh Grant (she did marry him at the end of the first movie) and he invites his mate Bernie, played by Bonneville, around for a social dinner. She does not know that he is now a peer and when she asks him what he does at the weekends, his response (to steal the memorable line of Maggie Smith who plays the Earl's mother in the TV series) is: 'What's a weekend?'

I know that this is all only drama dreamed up by screenwriters but the theme relates to real life too. Most people have their moment in the sun and as a friend of mine joked to me the other day: 'It's better to be a has-been than a never-was or a never-will-be.' At some stage, one must do just one remarkable thing that people will remember you by. Just once you need to be a recognisable star bathing in the adulation of maybe just the members of your immediate family. Then you can fade from view.

Spring is in the air, but which one?

If anything showed that the Arab Spring applies not only to dictatorships but also to democracies, it is its spread to Turkey, Brazil and yet again to Egypt. South Africa could have its own version if we do not take steps to match our political democracy with an inclusive economy.

I love spring. I can walk around my suburb in Johannesburg in shirt sleeves, the plane trees have new green leaves and the flowers are out in profusion. When spring is in the air it is a great time to be alive.

But there is another spring in the air too – the one that has happened in certain Arab countries to the north of us. At the beginning of June I wrote a column on the latest South African scenarios in which I said that one of the red flags for a "Failed State" scenario was high youth unemployment combined with active social networks combined with a growing alienation from the authorities by young people. This suggests that we were one random event away from our own version of an Arab Spring.

Could Marikana be that random event? We are seeing things happening which have never happened before. The mining industry is almost turning into a general rebellion not only against employers but against the unions too. Workers are discovering a new-found solidarity amongst themselves as they fight for better wages. Meanwhile, Julius Malema has become a politician and speaker addressing any group that has a grievance and saying things about our political leaders which not even the bravest commentators would say in public. The service delivery protests also seem to be ratcheting up to a new level as ordinary citizens are no longer afraid of the long arm of the law descending on them.

The anger and the vitriol of the comments on news websites are reaching new heights on subjects like employment equity on the one hand and how the political settlement in 1994 has proved to be totally disappointing in providing economic improvement for the vast majority on the other hand. It is almost open warfare on any controversial column written by News24 columnists or bloggers with an axe to grind. News developments are greeted by joy or derision depending upon which side you are on.

To put it mildly, the temperature in this country has risen by a substantial number of degrees and, as we all know, heat can produce some very intense reactions. I am sometimes criticised for putting the "Arab Spring" scenario on the table on the grounds that we are a democracy and the affected Arab countries were all dictatorships. My response is to point to the two days of mayhem in London last year when young people went on a looting spree and burnt down some significant buildings. Britain is a democracy and in a minor way had its own version of an Arab Spring. France, Spain and Greece are all trying to cope with a citizenry who have become increasingly restless as a result of austerity measures. They are democracies too.

All in all, we could be at a pivotal moment in our history where we could tip into the no-holds-barred anarchy of a "Failed State"; or we could accept that the game has to change in order to create an economic democracy that goes with our political democracy – in other words begin the process of transforming our economy into an inclusive one offering genuine economic freedom and the chance for ordinary people to better their lives and circumstances.

This cannot be done overnight but most people do not have that expectation. They want to see the arrow pointing in the right direction and incremental success being achieved. For some time I have been listing the initial steps that I would like to see being taken. They are as follows:

1 The holding of an Economic Codesa involving government, business, the unions, civil society champions, entrepreneurs, NGOs and ordinary citizens. A new blueprint has to be hammered out with give and take on all sides. It is a joint exercise, not the government handing down yet another plan.

2 A complete change in mindset towards small business and entrepreneurs where the bulk of the new jobs to bring down our unemployment rate to reasonable levels will be created. I attended a 702 small business awards ceremony and that is the future of South Africa. Like America, 70% of the top 100 businesses in 30 years time in South Africa should be relatively unknown small businesses today. Think about it – nobody knew about Microsoft when IBM was at its peak and nobody really rated Apple when Mircosoft was at its peak. You need the creative destruction of capitalism to produce a world class economy and that is not to be dismissed as a neo-liberal slogan.

3 A radical shift in black economic empowerment where workers have a real stake in the economy as opposed to a few favoured individuals. Every major company in South Africa should have an employee share ownership programme.

4 The government should concentrate all its energy on improving service delivery in education, law and order, health and all the other services that governments normally provide by hiring the right people for the right jobs. We must get rid of cadre deployment. They should as far as possible keep their noses out of business and

wealth creation because that is the domain of entrepreneurs. Equally, NGOs are superb at fighting the war on poverty but they do need the money.

I am sure there are other steps that I have forgotten which readers can add. The upside of what is happening now is that it must be seriously rattling the "establishment" so they should be more willing to entertain new ideas and take more risks. Necessity is the mother of invention so let's create a spring as good as Mother Nature.

Searching for Sugar Man

Isn't it nice that this movie went on to win the Oscar for best documentary at the 2013 awards ceremony?

Take the time to watch a movie called *Searching for Sugar Man* because it will give you an all-time high, particularly if you, like me, are a vinyl junkie (a collector of those prehistoric things called long playing records).

The film is about a singer named Sixto Diaz Rodriguez whose parents immigrated from Mexico to America. It is not just his music but his life which makes Rodriguez such an interesting person.

Born in 1942, he made two records – *Cold Fact* in 1970 and *Coming from Reality* in 1971. Neither record did particularly well in the US and he basically disappeared from the public eye soon after their release.

However, in South Africa he sold half a million records which put him ahead of virtually any artist on the planet. He was also popular in Australia and New Zealand. With rumours of his death circulating, two South Africans set out to uncover the mystery of his disappearance. One was a fan called Stephen "Sugar" Segerman and the other was a journalist called Craig Bartholomew Strydom. They even set up a website called The Great Rodriguez Hunt.

The film is about the surprising twists and turns that take place in the search for the singer in America, centred on Detroit in Michigan. I cannot possibly reveal the outcome because I had never heard of Rodriguez and it has to be one of the best plots I have ever come across – and I have seen a lot of movies in my life. In the *New York Times*, Manohla

Dargis called the film 'a hugely appealing documentary about fans, faith and an enigmatic Age of Aquarius musician who burned bright and hopeful before disappearing.'

Produced in a joint venture between the Swedish and British film industries, the movie premiered at the 2012 Sundance Film Festival in the US, winning its Swedish Director Malik Bendjelloul the Special Jury Prize and the Audience Award for best international documentary. It has also won awards at festivals in Los Angeles, Durban, Melbourne and Moscow.

After the movie, I immediately bought the two CD compilation at the record shop in the Zone in Rosebank. It is amazing. The guy sounds like a cross between Bob Dylan and Donovan and his songs about inner city life, especially what it is like to be poor, have an enduring quality. No wonder people in faraway countries went crazy about him just as the French went crazy for Johnny Clegg.

Last night, I was walking back to my hotel along the beachfront in Port Elizabeth. Passing a restaurant, I heard one of his songs being played to the clientele. It is called 'I Wonder' and the first verse came loud and clear through the windows (I kid you not):

I wonder how many times you've been had
And I wonder how many plans have gone bad
I wonder how many times you had sex
I wonder do you know who'll be next
I wonder I wonder wonder I do

As a scenario planner, I am constantly wondering about the future.

15 000 lives snuffed out

It is so tragic that we have such dreadful murder statistics, every one of which is a human being with the candle of life that burns once and is gone.

My grandfather was murdered in London while he was walking in the street during one of the blackouts during the Second World War. He was wacked on the head by a mugger and died of complications in hospital. One of my close colleagues in Anglo American, and probably the most brilliant corporate finance expert the company has ever had, was killed on his doorstep in Johannesburg.

The father of one of my daughter's friends was found in the boot of a burnt-out car in the Eastern Cape. The son of a relative of my wife, who was a lawyer and did charitable work in Hillbrow, was shot in cold blood. The young nephew of dear friends was lured out of a garden and killed in a coastal resort.

Life as a candle

With the exception of my grandfather, all the others had their lives prematurely ended during my lifetime and in South Africa. As for friends of friends, we have had two murders in Johannesburg this year. In how many countries anywhere in the world could you go to a dinner party where everybody at the table could recount similar stories? Certainly, in London I stuck out like a sore thumb with my grandfather's wretched demise. Nobody else had a single example.

I visualise the taking of life as candles being snuffed out. Each of us is a candle that is lit at birth. The little flame sputters and grows and for a time can provide light for an entire room. Then the flame gradually subsides and finally dies out when the wick is exhausted. It only happens once for every person, so they have to cast as much light as possible during that brief period and glow as intensely as they can – lighting up the lives of other people and particularly their families. Over a couple of generations, relatives and others may share memories about your life as a candle; but then you are forgotten forever unless you are very famous.

Every year in South Africa, more than 15 000 candles are snuffed out viciously by murderers. Black candles, white candles, coloured candles – that little flame at the top of the wax is extinguished in an evil and violent manner. Think of how much time it would take to snuff out 15 000 candles. In real life, think of the space that is occupied by 15 000 people: 10 office blocks, 50 planes, 100 hotels, a third of a rugby stadium. All gone. Numbers cannot express the loss. Each one is a human spirit.

A sad reflection

It just goes on remorselessly every week. Somewhere another candle, beloved by other candles, is rudely destroyed with the perpetrator walking away with his flame comfortably still lit. Before you say anything, I know that women commit murders too, but the vast majority are committed by young men. 'I am' because you are no more. What a sad reflection on human nature that you have to terminate somebody else's existence to affirm your own. Or else you just don't care.

Don't blame it on poverty and inequality. There are lots of poor people with proudly burning flames who would never dream of snuffing out another candle. They want their own and their loved ones' candles to burn as long as possible. Normal people do. They just live in constant fear of becoming the next statistic.

My Bucket List

As one gets older and life becomes finite, there are always things you want to see or experience in your remaining days or years.

The reason I am writing about bucket lists (things you want to happen before you exit this world) is that I can now cross off two items from my list as they have both happened in the last year.

1 My soccer club, Chelsea, winning the Champions League once in my lifetime. They did so in 2012 more as a result of luck than anything else but they did it. So for one year I have bragging rights and they are four points ahead of Manchester United at the top of The Premier League at the moment.

2 Seeing a leopard in the bush and being the first to come across it. That happened in the Pilanesberg and it has never happened to me before. I have seen an ear behind a rock as the tenth vehicle to enter the lock; but here in the evening sunlight was a young female leopard in full view crossing the road slowly and looking back at my binoculars before disappearing into the grass. If the vehicle had arrived a minute later, we would have seen nothing.

So, this got me thinking what else do I want that is unusual. Obviously, as a parent and a grandparent I want my children and children's children to do things I could never have achieved. Above all, I want them to be happy. But what are the other eight things that I would like to happen before I meet my maker?

3   I must take my wife on a trip to somewhere exotic which is a complete surprise. My visits to other countries have tended to be for family or business reasons. I have never done anything crazy like going on a yodelling tour in the mountains around Vienna. You are never too old to learn to yodel.

4   I would like the fox to be as iconic as the hedgehog in American leadership circles. Jim Collins won well-deserved praise for his book *Good to Great* which showcased the notion of having one big vision and focusing on it. I want to make the idea that you need the mind of a fox which picks up the flags of imminent change and has a quick response to them as popular as Jim's to be a visionary hedgehog. You need both qualities to feature as a good leader today, especially in these volatile times.

5   A cure for HIV/Aids during my lifetime definitely sits on my bucket list, having met so many exceptional people involved in the fight against this epidemic. I want to overcome the heartbreak of young kids having to look after families because both their parents have been killed by the virus.

6   I would like to see South Africa ranking alongside New Zealand, Finland and Norway as one of the least corrupt countries in the world. At the least the media here have put the issue of corruption and waste on the table. Now we need to get rid of it. Morality starts at the top.

7   I want one South African, black or white, to come up with one product that takes the world by storm and thereby to become the next Steve Jobs. Why should America have a monopoly on ingenuity? Chris Barnard had the whole world gobsmacked with his first heart transplant. We need a repeat which puts South African business firmly on a par with the best the US, Europe and Japan can offer.

8   One of my most passionate desires is for the mindset of

this country to change about entrepreneurs. If we want real economic democracy and freedom, it has nothing to do with changing the ownership of the mines and banks. It has everything to do with creating the space and the support system for small enterprise to flourish.

9   This may be a long shot, but a world-wide debate on where our planet is heading needs to take place. Can we afford 10 billion people by 2050 and if not, what are we going to do about it? Remember the first billion was reached just over two centuries ago. Our success at reproducing ourselves as a species has led to other problems – the disappearance of many other species and the imminent breakdown of large chunks of our ecosystem. There is no Plan(et) B.

10 I just wish the Proteas could be like Chelsea and win one Cricket World Cup without choking. We must congratulate them on being at the top of the rankings, but hey, you've got to win a grand slam event to be hailed as a superstar.

My bucket list may have a hole in it but that is my best shot at hopes before I shuffle off this mortal coil. The Proteas still have to surprise me with my tenth wish.

Looking over the edge of a cliff

The whole point of our methodology is that it is a dynamic radar system – like a fox looking constantly around a forest for potential opportunities and threats. The speed of response is critical before things move beyond your control.

Just over a year ago, Chantell Ilbury and I were giving a 70% probability to South Africa staying in the "Premier League", 30% to a peaceful decline into the "Second Division" and zero to a "Failed State". With the tabling of the Secrecy Bill, we changed to 50% for "Premier League", 40% for "Second Division" and 10% for "Failed State". Gagging the media would remove an essential pillar of democracy, precipitate a massive increase in corruption and terminate our brand of being a model for the rest of Africa to follow. Accordingly, we went more negative.

With the Marikana tragedy ushering in a period of industrial turmoil which, aggravated by the lack of service delivery, could escalate into a full-blown South African version of the Arab Spring, we have revised the probability yet again. While we are keeping "Premier League" at 50%, we now have amended the chances of a peaceful versus violent, anarchic decline from 40:10 to 50:50 and therefore accord the "Second Division" and "Failed State" scenarios each a 25% probability.

We have been saying for several months that South Africa shares the same characteristics as those existing in all Arab countries that have experienced or are experiencing a popular uprising: an abnormally high youth unemployment rate; combined with active social networks; combined with a growing alienation towards the state by young people. All these uprisings were triggered by a random event and maybe in our case it was Marikana. One senses a change in mood among the workers in this country. They no longer trust authority whether that authority is exercised by employers, the unions or the government. If that deep distrust and anger continues and merges with the total desperation felt by the unemployed, then we have a recipe for a revolution which nobody in authority will be able to control.

Hence, it would be foolish for Chantell and myself to continue backing peaceful decline into Third World status as our favourite downside scenario. Events have shown how quickly the wheels can come off when the mood turns ugly. However, we are at pains to emphasise that the incidents so far are relatively isolated and we are still a long way from the violence that engulfed Libya and is destroying Syria.

The whole point about scenarios is to recognise when the chandelier in the ballroom is beginning to tremble. The way we are programmed is to stick our heads in the sand and go on enjoying the party until the lights go out. Like everyone else, neither Chantell nor I wish to raise the probability of a terrible outcome. But the flags say otherwise and the purpose of flags is to take emotion out of our judgement on the probabilities of desirable and undesirable futures.

We are still holding the odds at 50:50 on "Premier League" versus "Second Division" and "Failed State". We still maintain that the country is at a tipping point where it can tip either way. What we are saying, though, is that the penalty for not tipping in the right direction has just become a lot more extreme. Have we as a people got a sense of crisis to remedy the situation? You decide.

As for Chantell and I as two seasoned scenario planners, we sense a perfect storm approaching which could blow us over the edge of the cliff. All around the world, inequality is increasing as technology drives a stake through traditional job creation and human greed ensures the rich get richer. South Africa just started higher up on the inequality scale. We need a new economic accord which gets rid of the waste, inefficiency and corruption. We cannot afford it anymore. We need to tighten anti-monopoly legislation to create the space for millions of new small enterprises. We need to return to a stable industrial relations climate by creating greater wage parity, better living conditions for workers and a greater sense of common purpose.

All this can only be achieved by setting up an Economic Codesa to come up with a new economic blueprint involving measurable outcomes for all the parties concerned – and to which they are held accountable by each other.

We are in a state of emergency. Collectively, we have to resolve it.

Mr President, you should lead by example

All of us look to our respective leaders to provide guidelines on how we should behave. A leader's example is more persuasive than any written code of conduct.

I have just read the following paragraph on News24: 'Zuma also called on senior officers in business and government to freeze salary increases and bonuses for the next year as a "strong commitment to build an equitable economy".'

I totally support the sentiment, but the President has to be the first in line by announcing what sacrifices he is personally going to make in order to get the show on the road. Genuine leadership is about action, not words. I wrote the following in an article after Warren Buffet called for the US government to get serious about shared sacrifice: 'Coincidentally, I have been saying the same for some time that Barack Obama should be leading from the front by taking a pay cut himself. He should insist that members of Congress do the same.'

For a start, I find it amazing how many members of government are allowed to travel business class on SAA. The other day, I remember seeing a prominent SACP individual in business class on his way to Cape Town when just on the other side of the curtain in economy sat the ambassador of one of those western capitalistic nations he so often derides. The ambassador told me that budgetary considerations now meant that all his diplomatic staff had to travel in the back of the plane.

As for hotels, the appalling stories in the press of senior government officials booking penthouse suites in the best hotels in London, New York and everywhere in South Africa make you wonder how such extravagance can be tolerated in these economic hard times. Sometimes the rooms are not even used. Ordinary folks now stay in budget hotels or bed and breakfasts to cut down the cost of travel.

Moreover, this belief that there is an endless stream of tax-payers' money swelling state coffers extends to flashy cars and bodyguards. Why is it that even at provincial and local government level senior employees are allowed to drive top-of-the-line models? I drive a 10-year-old Mini on trips around town and a Land Rover Discovery with the wheel on the back if I am going on holiday.

Blue light convoys and bodyguards are yet another example of total excess. Please give me one other country in the world where the leader of the ruling party's youth wing travels around in a convoy with a troop of bodyguards. Not even in Russia. Is South Africa so spectacularly dangerous that every single minister and every single senior party official has to be afforded the level of personal protection that they are given? I remember in Anglo American that the only person who had a bodyguard was Harry Oppenheimer, who successfully evaded him when he wanted to walk by himself to the barber in Commissioner Street.

We can widen the list of items to be trimmed to residences, conferences, overseas trips, the quality of whisky, you name it. The fact is that for a party that espouses left-wing ideology and calls for measures to narrow the gap between the haves and the have-nots, there is an Orwellian contradiction between the sacrifices being demanded of others and the sacrifices being made by the party itself. 'Some people are more equal than others' is the perception held by many members of the public.

Nevertheless, I shall heed the President's call. I solemnly promise that I will not put up my fees for my speaking engagements in 2013. Now I want to know what you are going to do, Mr President.

What does a 25% probability for a Failed State really mean?

It all comes back to you, your family, the organisation you work for, to decide what you are going to do. Scenario planning, as we have modified it, is anything but an intellectual exercise. It is the prelude to action.

Recently, I wrote a column for News24 raising the probability of South Africa becoming a "Failed State" to 25%. Subsequently, many people asked me what it means and what they should do about it.

Should I make sure my passport is up to date? Should I be going on an LSD (look, see, decide) trip to Australia? Should I be approaching a head hunter for job options in Europe? Should I legitimately be sending more money offshore to mitigate the declining rand? Should I be stocking food?

Connecting the dots

These are all valid questions which have been posed to me. Chantell Ilbury and I have always said that part of thinking like a fox is to connect the dots. You cannot just play scenarios – that's daydreaming. You have to consider your options for each scenario and then decide what you are going to do about it depending on the probability and impact of the scenario. You can either do something now or prepare a contingency plan just in case. Either way, the whole point of the process is to improve the speed and quality of your response in chasing the opportunities and countering the threats offered by the scenarios.

So, let's get back to the significance of a 25% probability.

Pictorially, it covers an "L" or 90 degrees of a circular disc. If you spin the disc, there is a one in four chance that the needle will end up on that 90 degree segment. What is more is that if you spin it again whatever the previous result, the probability is still one in four. Like spinning a coin where you get 10 heads in a row, the chances are still 50:50 that the next one will be a head. The difference between these examples and real life is that real life only happens once and therefore probabilities are far more subjective.

Recently, I had a discussion with a group from MIT in the US who tried to convince me that you can mathematically link the raising of the flags on our scenarios to their probabilities. I am not so sure because of the one-time aspect of life; and so much of what happens is due to the animal spirits or irrational nature of mankind.

The bottom line is that the 25% probability of a "Failed State" is instinctive and should be treated as such. In other words, there is nothing scientific about it and if you have a different figure in mind, you are quite entitled to base your actions on your figure not ours. Suffice it to say, in our mind, the "Failed State" scenario is no longer a wild card possibility lurking in the shadows: it is now a genuine threat, the consequences of which have to be thought through.

Impact of the scenario on you

This brings us to the second aspect that has to be considered which is the impact of the scenario on you as a business, you as a family or you as a person. If I said to you that the plane you had booked a flight on had a 25% probability of crashing, you almost certainly would not take it unless you were in a war zone and wanted to escape. The reason is a high likelihood of death in the event that the scenario materialises. Equally, if I gave you a 25% probability of being eaten by a shark when swimming off a particular beach, it would be very foolhardy of you to go in the water. One of the reasons you would not take the risk in either case is that the alternative options are usually easy to exercise: use another airline and go to another beach or swimming pool.

The impact of a "Failed State" scenario is far more difficult to imagine since so many varieties of a failed state exist, ranging from oppressive dictatorships through perpetual anarchy to civil war and at the extreme end genocide. No expert in the field here has adequately described the different forms that a failed state in South Africa could take. We certainly can't, particularly with regards to timing and rate of descent.

The only thing we can state with confidence is that the rest of the world will collectively turn its back on us, apart from a few outcasts who will welcome us to the club of pariah nations.

Two categories of options

Hence, the evaluation of the overall risk of this worst case scenario, namely probability times impact is a highly personal thing. And so too is the selection of options available which depends on individual circumstances such as age, level of wealth and education, business experience and skills, as well as the number of children and other family commitments you have in South Africa. In the case of a business, the opportunity to expand the geographical footprint outside South Africa will be linked to its range of products and services, health of its balance sheet and potential partners elsewhere.

However, options can be divided broadly into two categories: adapting your own strategies and tactics as regards your own future in light of the changing odds of the scenario; or rolling up your sleeves and taking action – however big or small it may be – to reduce the odds of the scenario itself. In other words, you become an active citizen in ensuring that South Africa does not fail.

Far be it from Chantell and myself to give you specific advice on which option you should take, what our 25% probability means is that you should give the matter some serious thought if you have not done so already. Then decide on appropriate action or have a contingency plan.

That is what a fox would do – logically not fearfully, with a sense of purpose, not despair.

Three foxy lessons from Superstorm Sandy

Catastrophic risk management is a discipline that will receive much more attention in future as extreme events increase in frequency. The quality of the immediate response to a crisis sets the tone for the treatment of the whole thing. You have to be prepared as best you can.

Sandy, the near-perfect storm that engulfed the north-eastern states of America, had quite a few messages which Chantell Ilbury and I have been trying to get across in the three books we have written together on foxes:

1 However powerful you are, there will always be events that are way beyond your control. Your only choice is in terms of the type, quality and swiftness of your response. How many people would have believed me if I had predicted that the financial centre of the United States – New York – plus a host of other cities in the region, would be shut down with empty streets, offices and shops. Foxes take dramatic action when it is required. They do not compromise when so many lives are at stake. They know precisely what they do and do not control. Above all, they recognise a problem when there is one.

2 However good a prophet you are, there will always be "black swan" occurrences that are unknown unknowns, things you don't know you don't know until they happen. All you can do is be a foxy script-writer and capture the possibility in very broad terms in an imaginative scenario; then work out a contingency plan and maybe carry

out simulation exercises with all the players involved; then act on the plan when the possibility in whatever form materialises. It is much better to be vaguely right than precisely wrong. You will never capture the future exactly. Foxes aim to be vaguely right, knowing that they will make some mistakes along the way which will serve as a learning experience for the next occasion.

3 Wherever possible, you should have a system of flags in place indicating the onset of a particular scenario and its probable evolution. In the case of hurricanes and tsunamis, the work has been done and the necessary sensory devices have been installed. Foxes will continuously upgrade their evaluation of an event using the information as it comes in and adapt their tactics as and when the need arises. Unfortunately, in man-made situations like the debt crisis in the Eurozone countries and in the United States itself, there is no map that can be shown on television indicating the progress of the storm and whether it is waxing or waning. Nevertheless, as best as you can, you have to develop substitute radar systems which can track an economic or political crisis and give you an intuitive feel of its range of consequences. Foxes are known for their bright eyes and quick instincts as regards the rising and falling of the flags. They are ahead of the herd in their response.

Americans have a growing respect for Mother Nature, particularly after the destruction wrought by Hurricane Katrina in New Orleans. They are getting better at handling natural disasters and cleaning up afterwards. I wonder whether they realise that the "fiscal cliff" they face at the beginning of a new year when national budget cuts are either imposed in a pre-set formulaic manner or agreed upon in a consensual manner by both houses in Congress poses an even greater danger to the country's future than any natural disaster. If there was a map devised by the economic equivalent of weather fore-casters showing the potential extent of the "fiscal cliff", it would cover the entire United States. Superstorm Sandy is a minor event by comparison.

Solely relying on The Fed to print extra dollars is not like emptying the streets. Indeed, it could even aggravate the storm! As I said, foxes recognise a problem when there is one. They do not ignore it and behave like it will just go away. They confront it as best they can with the resources they have at their disposal.

What, no crisis? You're kidding

People have every right to attach different probabilities and come up with different flags in respect of our scenarios. They can even formulate other scenarios which we have not imagined and thought through ourselves. The only request we make is that the behaviour of the person should be consistent with the probability that he or she assigns to the scenario.

Moreover, you should never let emotion or your current circumstances cloud your judgement about probabilities. Reversing the flow of logic and coming up with a probability which suits a decision that you have already made can prove fatal, particularly if the scenario is a negative one.

Since writing about South Africa looking over the edge of a cliff, I have had plenty of responses from: 'you should have said teetering" to: "anywhere but South Africa if you're thinking of investing in the continent of Africa.'

Nevertheless, the two comments I want to respond to are from respected members of the political and business establishments. Neither said it to me face to face; I read about their opinions in the media. The first stated that there was no crisis and there was no cliff, basically dismissing the idea of a 25% probability on a "Failed State". The second one said that South Africa has always lurched from one extreme to another, but we have always managed to right the ship and survive. Have a glass of nice red South African wine and think more hopefully about the future!

I beg to differ. Chantell Ilbury and I put the cat among the pigeons precisely because we believe the chances of a real crisis have risen dramatically (though we still give a 50%

probability to South Africa staying in the "Premier League"). Moreover, as the Titanic showed when five of its 16 watertight compartments filled up, there is a point of no return. We are just over one and starting to leak into the second compartment. Remember Egypt and Greece were the number one nations on Earth at some stage in ancient times. Now they are nowhere and Italy, formerly, Rome is heading in the same direction.

The assumption that South Africa will retain its premier status in Africa is distinctly dodgy, seeing how much our brand has declined. The dismal cover of *The Economist* featuring armed and angry mineworkers; the policy uncertainties around nationalisation, property rights and land ownership; the fraught relationship between striking workers, the unions, government and employees as well as the creeping anarchy that it has produced in the mining and agricultural sectors; the lack of leadership from the centre together with the unending stories of corruption and waste; the absence of any sense of crisis among many worthy members of the ruling class – all these factors have combined to produce a tipping point or, as I like to call it, a crossroads.

Back in the mid-1980s, Michael O'Dowd and Bobby Godsell as members of the Anglo scenario team produced a truly prophetic diagram on South Africa's transition from where it was at the time to South Africa becoming a modern democratic state and a winning nation. The first crossroads was the political one where we either negotiated a settlement with the real leaders like Nelson Mandela, or co-opted tame black representatives into a tricameral parliament. We took the "High Road" and came up with a world-class constitution, which led to a perfectly reasonable election in 1994.

The second crossroads was always the economic one where either we cemented our presence on the "High Road" with sensible economic policies that gained the approval of the majority of the electorate and the outside world; or we undid the entire progress we had made on the political front by adopting disastrous economic policies that caused us to swerve onto the "Low Road" of alternating populism and dictatorship – a pattern we called the Argentinian Tango.

South Africa is at that second crossroads where we either get our act together by having an Economic Codesa which establishes a consensus around what economic freedom really means and what the measures to make it happen really are; or we sink into an abyss where 'anywhere but South Africa' is the guiding principle for all those foreigners wishing to bet on Africa. We move from first to last in the minds of the world.

Wouldn't it be nice?

Sometimes, one has to come up with a personal wish list even if some of the wishes are beyond reach.

Wouldn't it be nice if:

- there were no suspicions or clouds around our President and he was seen as a totally honest, humble guy who lived in accommodation that most people found surprisingly modest;
- South African drivers realised that the left hand lane is the slow lane and not the lane for overtaking;
- the Springboks acknowledged that you only score if you have possession of the ball, the Proteas won one World Cup and Bafana Bafana recaptured the glory days of the mid-1990s;
- people from government arrived on time at meetings and did not send junior substitutes to speak on their behalf at conferences because they had to attend to more important matters of state;
- the government realised they are the servants of the people, not the other way around;
- CEOs were actually seen by workers walking the job, gathering opinions and showing some sense of humour;
- the Chinese discovered there was no medicinal value in rhino horns;
- you could see into neighbourhood gardens as no wall hindered your view from the road;
- good schools were praised for their outstanding results as opposed to being lambasted for the size of their classes;

- all our state hospitals were excellent enough for government ministers to use and all state schools were adequate enough for them to send their kids to;
- politicians travelled economy and collected their luggage from the carousel;
- if on one day all the robots in the entire nation were working at the same time;
- never again did you see a blue light convoy;
- never again did you have to tick a colour box when filling in an application for anything;
- 70 of the top 100 South African companies in 50 years time were not in existence today and were started by black and white entrepreneurs with ground-breaking ideas;
- just a few of our city streets were named after heroes in other arenas besides politics;
- a company announced that the income gap between its board and its workers had fallen as a result of a drive to share the pain of economic hard times;
- a party manifesto was published without any Marxist terminology or hollow-sounding rhetoric and instead consisted of measurable outcomes to improve the quality of life of ordinary people;
- the number of incidents of violent crime and murder in your suburb dropped so much that you took a bouquet of flowers around to the local police station;
- real life inter-racial relations were as good as those depicted in beer adverts;
- contracts were awarded to people who could actually do the job;
- all judges and state prosecutors were appointed on merit;
- those found guilty of corruption actually went to jail without medical parole;
- the lottery board were consistent in their donations to the NGOs which really make a difference;

- South Africa had its own Lula moment where it recognised its future rested on creating an all-inclusive, entrepreneurial economy;
- the government and unions understood that money does not grow on trees and revenue has to exceed costs for business to survive;
- every citizen was aware that South Africa has a fragile physical environment and a balance between it, economic development and human well-being is essential;
- the taxpayer was seen as a sacred cow to be milked at a reasonable percentage and not slaughtered by taxes, rates and tolls;
- the general state of living here was attractive enough to keep talented young South Africans away from thoughts of emigration, and our country was perceived to be the first stop for young, ambitious global citizens with dreams of being part of Africa;
- foreign companies and investors were welcomed warmly rather than treated with suspicion;
- the ruling party were more than a club where internal politics among the members superseded everything else, and instead they actually looked outwards;
- being South African, like being American, meant more to an individual than ethnic, racial or religious origin;
- we developed a "pay forward" mentality where philanthropy became a driving force among the more prosperous members of our community;
- we had an Economic Codesa which in retrospect was considered as the starting point for an economic democracy that became the envy of the world.

It would be nice, wouldn't it? And don't tell me to dream on!

Cyril is a flag

He is now Deputy President of the ANC and I wish him all the best.

When I was told of the possibility that Cyril Ramaphosa would be nominated as Jacob Zuma's deputy in the party and there might be a chance that the country's deputy position could be changed into that of Prime Minister, something went "ping" in my mind. This could signal a major shift in ANC strategy. After the next election in 2014, a scenario now existed that Zuma would become the equivalent of non-executive chairman of the country with Cyril as CEO.

This is not a bad idea even for those who passionately support the DA. The latter have virtually no chance of winning the next election as most pundits feel that they can only close the gap by 2019 or 2024. So one has to look at the best case scenario for the next seven or twelve years. Cyril, of course, has to overcome the perception among the masses of being a super-rich beneficiary of BEE and, more recently, of being a Lonmin Director when the company's role in the Marikana tragedy is under the microscope.

Nevertheless, I think if anybody can steer South Africa away from becoming a "Failed State" and towards a promotion in the ranks of nations that constitute the "Premier League", it is Cyril Ramaphosa. I have known him for many years after meeting him for the first time when he was General Secretary of the NUM. In those days, he wore a leather jacket and an NUM t-shirt and was a fiery, young advocate of all the rights that attach to being a mine worker. He fulfilled the position with great distinction and, to his credit, he never let the employing mines down by reneging on an agreement.

He established good relations with all the people with whom he negotiated and I remember he honoured an invitation by the head of the HR discipline in Anglo's Gold Division to attend his retirement party. This took place during the campaign leading up to the 1994 election. He could have easily passed it up, but he didn't.

Why do I think at this stage of South Africa's young democracy that he could play such a crucial role? Here are my reasons:

- He alone among prominent members of the ANC has open access to all the crucial players involved in our economy. He can ring any captain of the industry and ask him or her to attend a meeting and he or she will respond positively. With his union background, he can do the same with most unionists and clearly he can call upon anybody within the ANC. In other words, he has a unique networking skill;
- With Roelf Meyer, he was the engine room of the political Codesas we had in the early 1990s. If we ever decide to have an Economic Codesa, he could use all his experience to structure it in a way that maximises the chance of it being a success by extracting concessions on all sides; and
- Given his business experience and his track record in being the head of the appeal panel that heard the case of Julius Malema, he could instil real accountability within government and the ANC. Anybody who crosses the line would face instant dismissal from the party and potential criminal prosecution.

Thus, Cyril's nomination to a key ANC position is a very positive flag. I believe that this could transform foreign perceptions of South Africa being on a downward slide to nowhere. Instead, people might even talk of a second miracle being close at hand – the one that has to take place in the economic sphere.

21.12.12

I remember switching on the TV on 14 December 2012 and being overcome by the unfolding events at Sandy Hook Elementary School in Connecticut, which I talk about in a later column. Having written this one nine days before that tragedy, I realise that you can never capture an actual event in its precise form but you can have a vague premonition that something is in the offing.

In July 2005, Chantell Ilbury and I were asked jointly to facilitate a strategy session for one of Britain's largest companies at a venue near Glasgow in Scotland. As we were being driven back to the airport to fly down to London, I noticed a huge number of policeman stationed around the place. I asked the driver for a reason. Oh, he said, it is the G8 summit in Edinburgh and there have already been protests. Good time to attack London, he added, if you were a terrorist.

The following morning, I went for a walk from my hotel to Kensington Gardens and decided to get a cab back. There were no taxis around so I eventually walked back to the hotel. I said to the concierge that the congestion charge had obviously reduced the number of taxis on the road, and he replied that the reason was a power surge on the tube system. I thought how odd, and when I got up to my room I switched on the television to see if there was anything about it. The first thing I saw was a double-decker bus with its roof blown off. This was the morning when 52 civilians were killed by four suicide bombers on that bus and in the underground. Over 700 people were also injured.

At lunchtime, I walked across Westminster Bridge carrying my case to catch a train to Salisbury as the main line stations were re-opening that afternoon. Halfway across the bridge, I looked either way and I was the only object on the entire bridge. I wondered how often in the history of the bridge had there been only one person on it in the middle of the day. Very seldom and then two things struck me – what the driver said the previous evening and the fact that the day was the 7th day of the 7th month where the number 7 carries great significance for several religions.

Why tell this story? Because a significant date in the Mayan calendar is about to happen. On the 21st December 2012, the present era of Mayan history ended and a new cycle began. People have talked of the end of the world but actually it could be the beginning of a new phase of spiritual and physical transformation. Be that as it may, what concerns me is that terrorist movements know that this is a highly symbolic date and might be planning something somewhere. If you recall, Richard Reid tried to board a flight to America from Paris on December 21st 2001. He was the unsuccessful shoe bomber and because he only managed to travel the following night, the fuse in his shoe was too damp to ignite on account of rain and perspiration. That was a stroke of luck for the passengers on the same American Airlines flight.

Although the odds are low of another major incident, if I was a Western intelligence agency, I would be in a heightened state of alert and would be asking the public to have extra ears and eyes over the next 16 days. Anything suspicious should be reported and followed up. Earlier this year I met a group from MIT one of whom was a young woman who headed up the scenario planning team in Homeland Security in the US. I have a hunch the TV series called *Homeland* could be based on her as she was extremely bright. Anyway, we discussed whether scenarios should cover paranormal phenomena or just keep to the basics of envisaging rational threats. We decided that you have to cover all angles by putting yourself into the mind of the enemy, however wacky that mind is.

I sincerely hope 21.12.12 passes peacefully for all the inhabitants of this world and indeed a new era of constructive dialogue among warring nations is ushered in. But keep your fingers crossed.

Dear Mangaung Delegates

I wrote this article shortly before the ANC's national elective conference in Mangaung in 2012. The formula for a winning nation has not changed since it was first put on the table in 1987. The ANC must provide the environment in which South African citizens can make it happen.

Dear Mangaung Delegates,
All eyes in South Africa are on you as you wend your way to the ANC conference in Bloemfontein. Please heed the offer made by 33 of the country's top business leaders in an advertisement in a Sunday newspaper. I know many of them – they are people of integrity who have been successful on account of their talent at picking the right strategy and then, most importantly, turning that strategy into action.

Not one of them is trying to either manipulate policy in any particular direction or achieve any mischievous outcomes. All they want to do is assist you in converting your policy, as set out in the National Development Plan, into reality and turn South Africa into a winning nation. They have issued a call for action, of which they want to be a part, in order to overcome the one weakness this country has had for a long time: a penchant for producing fine plans but never implementing them properly.

We now have a common vision to create an economy three times the present size by 2030, while bringing down unemployment to 6% and making significant inroads on reducing poverty and inequality. Trevor Manual and his team of commissioners are to be congratulated on putting plenty of flesh onto this vision with their carefully constructed report. However, the government cannot make the vision happen by itself. It needs contributions from business, labour and civil society generally.

The business leaders undertook to promote 'a zero tolerance approach towards bribery, fraud and corruption and anti-competitive business practices'. Moreover they committed themselves to 'engaging with government and other public sector parties to foster ethical business behaviours necessary to create a modern, efficient and competitive economy that supports the growth of small, medium and micro enterprises which are crucial to job creation.'

Why don't you hold them to these words and, either through an established channel like Nedlac or through a new channel altogether, construct a series of measurable outcomes to which you can hold them - as well as the other parties involved – accountable? After all, the President has stated via his spokesperson that he will continuously engage business in the new year, and here is a golden opportunity to provide real substance to those engagements.

I would like, finally, to remind you what constitutes a 'winning nation' since it was the Anglo scenario team that first came up with the definition in 1987. There are six elements:

- **High education.** Standing on the brink of the knowledge-intensive 1990s, I used to emphasise that the foremost characteristic of a winning nation was the quality of its education system. Nothing has changed since then. If anything, the IT revolution has made the world even more knowledge-intensive.
- **Work ethic.** As I said at the time, it is not adequate to be knowledgeable: you have to work hard too, but there are four conditions for people to be willing to work hard. The first is small government. A marvellous Chinese proverb says: 'Govern a great nation like you cook a small fish:

don't overdo it'. The second, third and fourth conditions are a sound family system, low taxation and absence of corruption.

- **Mobilisation of capital.** Having people who are knowledgeable and work hard is not enough: one has to give them resources as well. This requires not only inducing a national savings habit but also putting in place a system that effectively delivers the savings to where they are most needed. In particular, the small business and informal sector should get their fair share.

- **Dual-logic economy.** As our team prophesised at the time, the new technologies would design both blue-collar and white-collar workers out of the system. They have since done so in virtually every developed and emerging economy in the world. Hence, there is a need to create a symbiotic relationship between the formal economy of big business and the informal economy of small business – especially via supply chain management schemes whereby small business manufactures components and big business assembles the final product. The logic of the two economies has to be integrated.

- **Social harmony.** You cannot have one half of a nation at odds with the other half. As we said at the time, you cannot have millions of angry black citizens but neither can you afford to have angry coloured, Asian or white citizens. You have to find something which satisfies South Africans as a whole.

- **Global player.** Lastly, as we observed, 'it is those nations that look outwards that win'. Nations that look inwards die. You have to play by the global rules of the game even if you are a superpower. And so for South Africa to bow out of the global race is the craziest notion of all. It still is.

There you have it. We can only become a winning nation by co-operating with one another. Please bear this in mind when you debate economic policy at the conference.

Yours sincerely,
A Patriot Fox

A case for gun control

Barack Obama has tried but not succeeded in making a significant difference because of opposition in Congress. The right to bear arms is so fundamental in the US that any attempt to modify it is rebuffed. Strange when the risks of a maniac going berserk as Adam Lanza did are as high as the Boston bombings which are classified as an act of terrorism. Both require maximum attention to prevent further casualties, especially as regards children.

In the chapter entitled 21.12.12, I reported on a conversation with a young American woman where we agreed scenario planning should extend beyond rational threats and 'that you have to cover all angles by putting yourself into the mind of the enemy, however wacky that mind is.'

Unspeakable evil

Since then, Adam Lanza aged 20 forced his way into the Sandy Hook Elementary School in Newtown, Connecticut and committed a crime of unspeakable evil. He shot 20 children and six adults before shooting himself. He also shot his mother at home. How do you in any way anticipate a crime like this? He lived in a decent suburb and though he had some mental problems, he did not have a criminal record. Nevertheless, what amazed me was that he had access to so many sophisticated guns alleged to belong to his mother. I wondered how many other houses in that suburb had an armoury like that.

To provide some context, I looked up some statistics on the internet. The US has 89 guns per 100 citizens versus 31 for Norway (where a crime of comparable evil was recently committed by a young man with guns) and 6 for England, Wales and Scotland. The right of people in America to keep and bear arms was ratified as the second amendment to their constitution in December, 1791. The gun lobby in America, principally represented by The National Rifle Association, is bigger and more influential than in any other nation. One only has to remember the Wild West where many men carried a Colt 45 in a holster on their hip and the fastest draw lived to fight another duel on another day. The right to bear arms is not just a legal clause. It is embedded in the history and culture of America.

So when Barack Obama says that something must now be done to reduce the frequency of these mass shootings (Columbine in 1999 and Virginia Tech in 2007 being previous examples) or eliminate them altogether, you have to say good luck to him. On the one hand, this is his second term and he can do unpopular things because he cannot be re-elected again. On the other hand, he faces immense resistance to any change in gun laws which reduce sales at a time when America is trying to climb out of the great recession.

The only answer

The problem is that technology has now produced semi-automatic and automatic weapons which can fire multiple rounds per second. Even a bad shot can inflict a lot of damage in an extremely short time, which is why these weapons are banned in many countries. The police in Newtown reacted with commendable swiftness but they could not stop the slaughter.

Gun control is the only answer to reduce the probability of such a scenario. But then it has to be universal so that it is not only the good guys that give up their guns. That will just make them more vulnerable. Harsh penalties must force the bad guys to cough up guns on the banned list too. They have to be treated like chemical weapons – a total no-no carrying a life sentence.

I know the argument will be put forward that Scotland with a figure of six guns per 100 citizens had its own school massacre at Dunblane in 1996, but if you have a better idea than gun control, please put it forward. For me, it is the only way for the most powerful nation on Earth to stop inflicting such enormous harm on itself. Go for it, Barack.

Five leadership lessons for 2013

A good interviewer brings out the best in the people he or she interviews, not by shirking the tough questions, but by establishing some kind of rapport with the person interviewed. Bruce Whitfield, with a combination of wit and knowledge, never fails. In his own way, he is a leader by the questions he asks.

During an interview on 702 at the end of 2012, Bruce Whitfield asked me what principal lessons on leadership were learnt in 2012 which might be carried into the future. There were five I quoted:

1. Co-operative leadership

It is a global rule of the game under all economic scenarios that to get things done, you need co-operation from people or parties you don't control. Whether it is the ANC needing the co-operation of business, unions and civil society to implement the National Development Plan; or whether it is President Obama needing the co-operation of Congress to avoid the fiscal cliff: in both cases neither the ANC nor Obama can go it alone. The ANC requires the support of business just as Obama needs the support of the Republicans. It may be a drag to be nice to people that you normally can't stand, but that is the way it is in today's world.

For this reason alone, Mangaung has made me feel a lot better than before. The election of Cyril Ramaphosa to Zuma's deputy in the ANC is a signal that the government realises that to implement a common vision for this country, which genuinely achieves a better life for all, it requires a joint effort by all players. We are moving from walking behind each other to walking together. Hurray!

2. Problem-solving leadership

2012 was the year of kicking the can down the road and not addressing the fundamental sovereign debt problem besetting the rulers of the biggest economies in the world. The central banks are printing money like fury to buy up the bonds being issued by governments and to keep interest rates as low as possible. The Bank of Japan now owns 11% of its nation's outstanding debt; the US Fed is purchasing 40% of all American treasuries auctioned at the moment; and the European Central Bank has pledged to buy unlimited quantities of Spanish and Italian bonds. Lucky for all of them, inflation has not reared its head above 3%.

Are they resolving the problem? No way. They are buying time for the politicians to get their financial house in order by either raising tax revenues or cutting government expenditure or both – the only real solution to a budget deficit and towering debt. However, austerity measures are unpopular with the electorate and so the can gets kicked further down the road. At some point, the can grows to a size where it can no longer be kicked. Ireland, Britain and Greece are finally taking the right medicine but will America, Italy and Spain follow? Or will they bring down the whole house of cards because, like the commercial banks once appeared to be, the misperception exists that they are 'too big to fail'.

3. Leadership by example

In these hard times, how many political and business leaders have practised austerity measures on themselves by taking salary reductions, cancelling Head Office festive functions in line with the operating business units, trying to keep employees in jobs as opposed to keeping them in a permanent state of uncertainty about forthcoming retrenchments, showing generally that leaders are capable of sharing the pain?

Somehow we have to recapture the spirit of the festive season in terms of generosity and doing unto others what we would like them to do for us if we were placed in a similar, miserable position. It is not all about the bottom line and growth and efficiency and pleasing the analysts. Only good old morality and spirituality will allow us to kill the three-headed monsters I call PIU - poverty, inequality and unemployment.

4. Knowledge leadership

Knowledge of the game transcends culture and affiliations. Gary Kirsten led India to become the number 1 test cricket-playing nation and now he has done the same for South Africa. Other than at one time sharing the characteristic of being a member of the British Empire and now being democracies, these two nations have marked cultural differences: yet one man could take 11 individuals in each nation and mould them into a victorious, fighting machine on the cricket pitch.

This type of leadership is all about understanding strategy and tactics of the game because you have been involved in it for a long time. Experience counts and so does bringing out the best in the players. It would be nice if our government understood this principle when appointing the CEOs of para-statals: they must have a knowledge of the game that only comes with experience. Cadre deployment is like making Gary Kirsten Springbok rugby coach because of his services to cricket. He won't get the same results, however good his general leadership qualities are. It's a different game.

5. Get-up-and-go leadership

One of the highlights of 2012 is that we are beginning to see the emergence of entrepreneurial leadership in South Africa where individuals just get up and go and do their own thing. By so doing, they become local heroes as one TV campaign has testified in covering the remarkable ascent and contribution of people who have come from nowhere to secure their names in the annals of the community in which they live. Whether it is helping to start a cycling academy in Khayelitsha which has already produced some racing aces, or establish a conservatoire in Soweto which has allowed Rosemary Nalden to assemble an orchestra which plays all over the world; or whether on the business front it is creating Fundamo based in Cape Town which is now the world's leading specialist mobile financial services solutions provider – all these examples are setting the scene for South Africa to become the leading nation in innovation in the Southern Hemisphere.

Whenever I fill in one of those tedious visitor books at the reception desk of a big corporation and they ask me what company I work for, I put "myself". Oh that the government here understands that creating five million jobs by 2020 means backing one million new get-up-and-go business and social entrepreneurs. They'll do the job of creating five million jobs, no problem.

If as a reader you have managed to get this far in the chapter, I wish for 2013 to be for you "The Sweetest Thing", to quote the name of the best patisserie in Simon's Town.

Two real game-changing flags

One of the terrible things I have found is that the more successful a company is in its current game, the more blind it is to the flags that are changing it. On-line shopping is transforming the High Street and on-line reading is changing the way we assimilate information. Businesses not adjusting to the new reality will become extinct. Foxes always have one eye cocked on changes taking place in the business environment – and, boy, did a big flag rise on a major change which is turning the retail sector upside down. Since I wrote this column, Jeff Bizos, the founder of Amazon.com, has bought The Washington Post. Now that signals a new game in the newspaper trade.

John Lewis, a major UK retail chain, announced that online Christmas sales in 2012 were 44% higher than the previous year. Now I know that online sales are still a relatively small proportion of overall retail turnover in most countries, but this result was sensational when Christmas sales for the whole of the UK were almost flat. Significantly, most major brand retail groups in the UK recorded online sales growth in double figures though I haven't heard of any others that rivalled John Lewis.

Here, in South Africa, I haven't seen any Christmas figures but I bet you we are experiencing the same phenomenon because we have the same reasons for converting to online shopping:

- it is more convenient for you as a customer and saves time;
- it is more cost-effective because you don't have to drive

or take public transport to the shop and then pay for expensive parking; and

- the actual price of the product you are purchasing online may well be cheaper than the identical product in a physical shop as the vendor is basically selling to you wholesale and is saving on the normal rental for retail space.

The only offset for the company selling you the product is that it pays the cost of delivering it to you. However, most online sellers (including online book marketers) have developed slick distribution systems. Yes, there are exceptions where people have had to wait an inordinate amount of time for delivery but as the online retail industry grows up, the problems will be ironed out.

Of course, retail foxes are already adapting to the new reality and John Lewis is leading the pack. In Australia, I went into a men's outfitters in Perth to check out some suits. The assistant sauntered over and said it would cost me 25 Australian dollars to try one on (that is R225). I said 'you're kidding', and he replied: 'I'm not. Most customers come in and try my suits on and buy the exact replica on the internet where you don't pay GST. So we've turned ourselves into a trying-on shop!'

The second game-changing flag fluttering in the wind came out of a conversation I had at a lunch in Somerset West. One of the guests who works as a reporter at a Cape newspaper described the significant cutbacks that have been made in the number of staff in newsrooms around the country. It means less specialisation and fewer reporters covering a greater variety of topics. Forensic investigation is almost becoming a thing of the past.

Online media sites like the one I write on are playing havoc with the business models of the printed media since you can get your news for free on the internet. Moreover, you can comment on it as a reader immediately which you cannot do in a broadsheet or tabloid. Virtually every newspaper in the world is therefore putting as much effort into its online website as it is into the paper itself. Yet, the majority of them are still offering content for free on the internet. Hence, the pressure on newspaper staff complements caused by pressure on profit margins.

Retail property developers and newspaper proprietors have to be really foxy in coping with the two flags I have described. Basically they have to reinvent their product, the former by turning their malls into an entertainment space (for example you cannot eat at an online restaurant) and the latter by offering more sophisticated commentary and analysis on the news rather than just breaking the news itself. My advice to both of them: stay bright-eyed and bushy-tailed as the High Street will never be the same again.

Will Australia become uninhabitable?

As the final column in this book demonstrates, it is not just Australia that is suffering the effects of the climate change we are experiencing.

Several years ago I was asked to facilitate a session of climate change experts in London on possible scenarios relating to how the issue would be tackled in the first half of this century. Two participants were key advisers to the US Senate and one was the principal adviser to the British Prime Minister at the time. In other words, it was a gathering of heavy hitters.

Two scenarios were offered post the Bali Conference: "Dances with the Wolves" where an agreement was hastily put together and promptly ignored by the super-emitters like America and China; and "Strictly Ballroom" where a tight agreement with measurable outcomes was formulated and everyone fell in line. The experts gave a 90% probability to the first scenario and only 10% to the second one playing out in the time period. In retrospect, their odds were right on the nose.

What intrigued me was the answer I got to a fundamental question I put to them: how certain are you that man-made climate change is for real? The response was this: there will never be 100% mathematical certainty on an issue like this, but as far as scientific certainty was concerned, we are prepared to give it a 95% probability, namely close to that needed for a legal conviction where the prerequisite is 'beyond reasonable doubt'. As one of them said: 'Judging by the evidence, I would put the climate change hypothesis on a par with Newton's Laws of Mechanics where the basic propositions will remain valid; but the principles may be modified just as

Einstein modified Newton's equations with the special and general theories of relativity.'

The other unforgettable point that was made at the meeting was that it was almost impossible to give credibility to climate change when it came to addressing the public. Talking of small increments in the amount of carbon dioxide in the atmosphere and small changes to the mean temperature of the planet made no mark because these phenomena were invisible. The only factor which could sway the public was the climatic VIX factor or volatility index possibly jumping to a much higher level; and weather extremes like hurricanes, cyclones, super-storms and extended periods of massive heat or chill – and rainfall or drought – becoming a more regular feature of our lives. As one representative said at the meeting: 'Seven Katrinas in a row flooding seven different cities in the US would definitely raise the issue to an appropriate level in the public consciousness.'

Maybe, the hammer has fallen, but it is not in the US – it is in Australia. The searing temperatures there, and the resultant bush fires must have precipitated a revival in the debate over global warming. At the best of times, Australia is a tough place to live from an environmental point of view. I remember taking a light aircraft into the Kimberley Plateau in the North West and landing in an area where the temperature occasionally approaches 50°C. We had lunch in a farmstead with an especially thick ceiling to counter the heat. Nothing can prepare you for walking in that type of inferno and any outdoor hike must be very brief to survive it.

Equally, reports have been coming in of abnormally high temperatures in the ocean driving sharks into the relatively cooler water closer inshore. Having been the "lucky country", Australia could be turned into the unluckiest country of all by Mother Nature. There's no such thing as outside air conditioning and the higher the temperature, the greater the evaporation of the limited water resources Australia possesses. Australia's population has more than doubled since the Second World War to a figure approaching 23 million. Jared Diamond, in his book *Collapse*, reckoned Australia had a sustainable capacity of around 8 million. He could have been prophetic for a reason he did not cite in his text.

The experts I referred to earlier made one further observation. They said there will be huge winners and losers as a result of climate change. However, it is too early to identify which nation falls into which category as computer modelling cannot handle all the complexities involved in regional predictions. What interests me is the response of the US and China in curbing their emissions if Australia is the fall guy. Getting the commitment of your own population to solve another country's problem is a tricky exercise. But the debate should start now.

1942, 1982 and perhaps 2012

Besides the point that I attribute to Warren Buffett at the end of this article, he also said that stock markets are totally unpredictable and any purchase of shares you make should be made on the assumption that you are acquiring the entire company. It gets you to burrow down into the data of a company's performance and prospects in a way that you would not do otherwise. Warren is a silver fox par excellence!

Notice the pattern. Three different years – 40 and 30 years apart: but what was the significance of 1942 and 1982? Both years were the start of huge bull runs in the Dow Jones Industrial Average: the first took the Dow from 100 to 1 000 in 1966. Thereafter it was flat until 1982 when it ascended to 12 000 in 2000. The first run was a multiple of 10 and the second was a multiple of 12.

Before 1942, the Dow was 100 in 1906. It rose to just under 400 at its peak in 1929, fell to 40 in 1932 and recovered to 100 in 1942. In other words, the overall result was flat for 36 years before lift-off in 1942. Between 1966 and 1982, the Dow oscillated between 600 and 1 000 before the second ascension to 12 000.

Why is this relevant? Between 2000 and 2012 the Dow rose to 14 000 in 2007, fell to 6 500 in early 2009 before climbing back to 12 000 in 2012. If you had got your timing right and bought after the Crash of 2008, you would have nearly doubled your money. By contrast, as a long-term investor, you would have experienced a glorious "U" ending up where you started in 2000. The same is true of the Standards & Poor's Index which started and ended at 1 500.

The million dollar question is this: have we had the oblig-atory resting period as what occurred before 1942 and 1982, implying that, based on historical experience, the Dow is now lifting off to a level of 120 000 by say 2030? The strength of the US stock market so far in 2013 – where the Dow has already touched 14 000 – would suggest that some kind of lift-off has occurred as a result of less volatility and better-than-anticipated corporate results. Thus, the second question is: can it be sustained or is this just another rally that will turn into another dip or, worse still, be the forerunner of another crash?

Let's start by going back to 1942 and 1982. Could you have recognised that either year was the beginning of a long-term boom in equities? 1942 was smack in the middle of the Second World War and the tide had not convincingly turned against Germany. Defence procurement was certainly helping Ameri-ca's economy revive from the Great Depression as was re-cruitment into the armed services. A clever American analyst might have spotted the turn, but would have had to have made the assumption of victory in the war (though of course Germany and Japan as the losers also made an incredible comeback in the 1950s).

1982 was in retrospect the year when another battle turned in favour of Western governments, this one being the battle against raging inflation. It did not take long to get down to reasonable single digit figures, but there was one character-istic shared between 1982 and 2012: negative real interest rates. Nobody wanted to keep money on deposit at banks or invest in triple-A bonds then and the same applies now as it is a recipe for losing the purchasing power of your wealth. Yet the driving forces behind the extended boom in the 1980s and 1990s were also the rise of the East and the IT revolution which produced the PC, the internet and the mobile phone.

So, beyond negative real interest rates, what other factors could sustain a long-term ascent in the Dow post 2012? I think the biggest plus is the possibility of another technological revolution but this time centred on improving energy efficiencies and coming up with completely new sources of energy. I would not be surprised if home-based solar energy systems, providing all the electricity needs of a household, will by 2030 be as common as mobile phones. Equally, the rise of the East may be supplemented by the rise of the South, namely South America and Africa.

On the minus side, two major restraints on the Dow accelerating upwards over time exist. First, and weighing heavily on any major recovery, is the megatrend of ageing populations in Europe and Japan and later down the line the demographic cliff faced by China as a consequence of its implementation of a one-child policy in 1978. America, India and other members of the developing world still have relatively young, growing populations which may to a certain extent offset this megatrend. The second downer is the fact that most over-indebted countries including America have made no inroads into correcting their budget deficits and reducing their national debt-to-GDP ratios. At some stage, action has to be taken or else another financial panic will ensue which this time is caused by worthless sovereign debt as opposed to sub-prime mortgages.

The markets are betting on a "Goldilocks" strategy in the US where the cuts are fine-tuned to a point that the problem is resolved without choking off economic growth. The porridge is not too hot and not too cold. It is definitely a flag to watch. Meanwhile, I believe the best approach to managing one's wealth is to have one-third in cash and bonds, one-third in physical property and one-third in equities (something my father taught me). Every two years, you reduce the category that has outperformed the others and increase the ones that have underperformed so you are back to a third, a third, a third. By all means, pick your own review period – some people prefer five years.

Essentially, this method mirrors Warren Buffett's advice to be greedy when others are fearful and fearful when others are greedy, because you are selling stuff that has done well and buying stuff that has done badly. You are diversified and contrarian at the same time. You will never do as well as a hedgehog who bets everything on a bull run and is right.

Nevertheless, by being a fox, you will never do as badly as a hedgehog who is proved wrong. And, by using this method, you make no assumptions about the future as the re-arrangement of your portfolio is determined by past performance.

The silent death of the private sector

This is a pretty brutal piece, but the trend towards the state providing most of the new jobs is not sustainable. Taxpayers' money to pay the salaries of the additional employees has its limits and South Africa's unemployment rate will only fall dramatically with a renaissance of the private sector.

Communists in South Africa must be popping the corks of their champagne bottles as they witness the dream of a state-run economy coming true. Socialists must be wearing a wry smile as, despite their belief in a mixed economy, they do have reservations about the profit motive. Why all this celebration? Because the big picture suggests that, with some illustrious exceptions, the decline and fall of the private sector is happening before our eyes.

The flags are going up everywhere:

- South Africa is no longer seen as the premier investment destination in Africa. The World Bank's list of fastest growing economies over the next five years has seven African countries in the top ten. They are embracing free enterprise while we continue to be dogged by policy uncertainty and increasing bureaucracy.
- Graphs shown by economists at seminars indicate the destruction of jobs in the private sector over the last five years offset by growing public sector employment and government grants. In January 2013, the overall drop of 50 000 jobs countrywide hardly dented the stock market or merited any press comment. In America, the Dow

would have fallen 5% on the news and the President would have been furious.

- The hikes in electricity tariffs – past and future – are completely undermining our competitiveness as a nation. Meanwhile, the country's flagship project – Medupi which is also the largest project in the Southern Hemisphere – has had no construction activity for over a month. Any hopes of the private sector having access to greater electricity supplies in the near future are currently being dashed.
- New small business formation has stalled as a result of lack of support for entrepreneurs and over-regulation. At the same time, many small businesses are going bankrupt on account of an inconsistent payment culture in government and big business. For many in the union movement, entrepreneurs have no right to exist as entrepreneurship does not amount to decent work. As members of the tripartite alliance, they can adversely influence the ruling party's attitude to small business.
- Cadre deployment and corruption have shut down many opportunities for the real stars in the private sector to be awarded state contracts. Equally, the cost of maintaining and building new infrastructure has gone through the roof, further undermining the cost-efficiency of the private sector.
- Hard times in the global economy combined with the growing anarchy in the workforce (where even established unions are no longer listened to by employees) have seriously squeezed many of our resource businesses which are a prime element of our economy. Even the largest companies in South Africa have limited cash reserves and borrowing facilities. If exhausted, they go bust.
- Unrestricted imports are causing havoc in our textile and food industries, lowering production capacity and mak-

ing the nation more reliant on the private sectors of other countries. Farmers are dreading land reform and selling up.

I could go on, but I think I have given enough examples to show that something is rotten in the state of South Africa.

We need to reverse the downward slide immediately. The only way we are going to do that is by having an Economic Codesa with measurable outcomes. Please, Cyril, step up to the plate. If you want to triple the size of the economy by 2030 and reduce unemployment to 6% – which is the objective of your and Trevor's plan – you have to have a thriving private sector. But you know that already.

How to implement the National Development Plan

So often worthy people put together a splendid plan but simply do not make the effort to propagate its contents to the people who will make it happen. Yet without the will and a programme of implementation, a plan is worthless. You have to stoke up the emotions of the public and make them passionate about its success.

Sometimes I go to a function not knowing what to expect but come away totally exhilarated. Such was the case last Friday at an event which celebrated International Women's Day. I was asked to be a panellist at the Women's Forum at Citi South Africa which was held in their offices in Sandton. It consisted of members of staff, mainly women but with a sprinkling of men. My fellow panellists were Devi Govender as MC, the intrepid journalist for Carte Blanche, and Jerry Vilakazi, business leader and member of the National Planning Commission. The topic chosen was the National Development Plan (NDP).

The following points emerged from the lively discussion with much audience interaction towards the end:

1 The NDP is a plan drawn up by South Africans for South Africans. It is not a government-formulated document. It comprises a diagnosis of our problems and then a series of steps to resolve them up to the year 2030. Poverty, inequality and unemployment are the root cause of our society's ills and chief among the targets set is to reduce unemployment to 6% by 2030 by creating another 11 million jobs to go with the 13 million we already have.

2 The ANC Conference at Mangaung in December 2012 universally supported the NDP as the way forward. It has now been adopted as official government policy and the five-year plans of individual government departments now have to register how they are going to contribute to the achievement of the plan in its first phase. It is acknowledged by senior ministers that critical to the success of the plan is the elimination of corruption and wastage, transparent tendering procedures where the best company wins and cost-effectiveness as an essential driving force in implementing the plan. Several ministers have already made it clear that they will not tolerate the status quo and heads will roll when they encounter opposition to change.

3 The NDP calls for active citizenry in the plan's implementation. Yet, from the audience's response, there is widespread ignorance of the plan's content and also a scepticism about its probable success given the current absence of proper service delivery at so many levels of society. Also, no sense of excitement has been generated around the NDP amongst the public despite the passion of the President and individual ministers for it. In order to achieve popular participation in the plan's delivery process, two essential steps are required:
- An information blitz across all media platforms (printed, TV, radio, the internet etc.) and in all indigenous languages simplifying the content of the NDP and making it readily understandable. Even reality TV programmes showing people doing their bit could be considered.
- Identifying a few easily implementable initial steps that can build the momentum in achieving the objectives of the plan during the first few years and making sure that those short-term goals are met and highly publicised. The plan is not all talk.

4 It is recognised by the compilers of the NDP that 90% of the jobs to be created by 2030 to bring the unemployment rate down to 6% will be in the small enterprise sector. However, both the panel and the audience recognised that the current environment for new entrepreneurs to emerge is not favourable for two reasons: the highly consolidated nature of South Africa's economy where much of the space is dominated by big business. We are no longer a frontier economy with low barriers of entry in the mining, manufacturing and service sectors. Secondly, a whole series of factors such as bureaucratic over-regulation; the absence of prompt payment for services rendered by entrepreneurs to government and big business; labour laws that are too rigid; the difficulty of accessing capital to finance small new ventures; and, critically, the lack of support for emerging farmers in the rural areas combine to make it almost impossible to visualise an entrepreneurial revolution taking place. These obstacles have to be addressed.

5 While everyone accepts that unions are part and parcel of a modern economy, it is envisaged that aspects of the NDP will meet stout resistance from the union moment. Bear in mind that the vast majority of jobs to be created will, to begin with, be non-unionised and therefore will not swell union membership. Only those companies that progress to the status of medium to large enterprises will eventually be unionised. Thus, the government as the elected body of the people will have to play a critical leadership role in allaying union concern and may at times have to show determination that the NDP must not be undermined from any quarter. Showdowns are possible and the government should not flinch as the prime organ of democracy from keeping the NDP on track.

6 The success of the NDP will be significantly enhanced if the private sector – and particularly big business – enthusiastically endorses it and participates in its implementation. If government is unwilling to call for an Economic Codesa at this stage, perhaps the CEOs of the major companies that make up the South African economy should organise a summit of their own to provide the clout that the plan needs to get the show on the road. As one participant enquired, why not overcome the natural tendency of South Africans to walk behind government and for once in one's life walk in front? Another suggestion was that each major company should call "town hall" meetings with its employees to identify those areas where the company could maximise its contribution to the NDP.

All in all, I walked out of the Citi Women's Forum feeling a lot more motivated about the future of this troubled land than when I walked in. Judging from the enthusiastic applause at the end, I think the rest of the people in that room felt the same. The NDP should move beyond a document for debate to a blueprint for action.

Boom! The threat of a nuclear conflict

Scientific discovery can never be reversed. The great quantum physicists of the 21st Century invented a monster of a device if put in the wrong hands – the nuclear bomb. We know what damage such a bomb can do and it is almost impossible to stop the proliferation of the knowledge needed to manufacture it. The genie is out of the bottle.

In our 2005 book *Games Foxes Play*, Chantell Ilbury and I provided 'The Ultimate Gameboard' because 'it is well known that the current nuclear weapons stockpiles of the few nations who have them are enough to destroy all life on this planet many times over. The future of our existence hangs in the balance, because access to these weapons could dramatically increase over the next fifty years.' Moreover, 'given the tempestuous nature of man, and his propensity for fighting, our world has been, and always will be, pockmarked with skirmishes, battles and wars that dictate the course of history'.

The four corners of the ultimate gameboard

We had four quadrants on our ultimate gameboard depending on whether peace (unlikely) or war would reign for the time being and whether or not nukes would be used in the next major conflict if and when it happened. One of the two peaceful quadrants we named "The Madhouse" where 'the logic is that mutually assured destruction (MAD) will deter any nation from a first strike. Obviously, the advent of stateless terrorism has knocked this principle on the head since terrorists who plant nukes need have no fear of reprisals in a specific spot'. The other quadrant we called "All Together

Now" where a new non-proliferation agreement is signed which lowers nuclear stockpiles worldwide and this reduces the threat of a nuclear exchange.

"Conventional Carnage" was our first scenario on the war side of the gameboard. For example the conflict in Syria would be included in this quadrant. The second we named "Boom!" and included potential nuclear flashpoints in Israel, Iran, North and South Korea and Kashmir. As we said, 'The "Boom!" zone has only been entered twice – on both occasions by America in Japan.' We also entertained the situation 'where some shady member of the arms trade passes on a nuke for $25 million to a terrorist outfit. It could have been manufactured in a private laboratory in a secret location. And James Bond does not come to the rescue.'

Two nuclear flags

The red flags on "Boom!" are rising. In a press briefing in Israel both Barack Obama and Benjamin Netanyahu agreed that Iran is now within twelve months of developing sufficient enriched uranium for a nuclear bomb as well as the delivery system (a missile) to go with it. The clock is ticking and the two leaders were at pains to say that no option, including the military option, could be ruled out. My gut feel is that Iran is not going to be deflected in any way from its nuclear programme particularly as Israel already possesses nukes. So a military showdown is more or less inevitable but whether that will involve nukes or conventional weapons is debatable. It could well be a pre-emptive strike by Israel using conventional weapons to knock out Iran's enrichment facilities. However, that may not succeed because the equipment used to manufacture enriched uranium may well be located deep underground in a highly fortified site.

The other red flag is North Korea which already has nuclear weapons and has recently tested them. They have just torn up

159

all agreements with South Korea and are threatening American bases in and around Japan. The young leader, Kim Jong-un, is proving to be even more belligerent than his father and it must be borne in mind that Seoul, the capital of South Korea, is close to the North Korean border and is a highly vulnerable target with about 26 million people inhabiting the metropolitan area. It is the second largest megacity on Earth behind Tokyo. Despite overtures from China designed to defuse the situation, again a showdown may not be avoided.

Conclusion

A nuclear exchange need not lead to the all-out nuclear war which has long been punted as the worst-case scenario. Nevertheless very foxy thinking will be required among the principal players to lower the risks of the nuclear game. We are indeed in extraordinary times. The stakes could not be higher.

Punish the saver, bless the borrower

As a saver, I have to confess to partisan feelings when writing this article. However, plenty of savers agreed with me in the comments column that accompanies every piece I do for News24.

To use a Yorkshire expression: 'The world is daft except thee and me, and sometimes I worry about thee.' In this case, 'thee' is Ben Bernanke.

There is a classic macroeconomic equation I learnt in my economics course at university: savings equals investment. If individuals and companies don't save out of their income, if governments don't generate surpluses in their annual budgets and if foreigners don't put some of their savings into your country's economy, then you don't have money to invest in new infrastructure, plants, machinery and new business ventures. Think about yourself: if your current expenditure equals your current income and you are putting no money to one side, investing in property, stocks and bonds is something you can do in your imagination, but not in reality.

Hence, I have always thought of saving as not only a virtuous activity (something my father lectured me on as well) but also a necessary condition for a healthy economy. Paul Samuelson, the great American economist, would I am sure be nodding his head in approval as it was his textbook that was the foundation of all economic learning at the time I was a student. So I am totally baffled by the economic policies pursued in the advanced economies over the last twenty years which have progressively discouraged people from saving and sometimes penalised them as well (such as negative interest rates in Japan occasionally making you pay to have money on deposit at the bank).

The tightening noose on savers

It all started with capital gains, interest and dividends becoming taxable in many countries, even though the capital invested had already been taxed at source. Up to a point I suppose you can justify that, especially when you hear Warren Buffett has one of the lowest rates of personal tax among his company's workforce. The reason is that most of his income is investment income. Then Alan Greenspan came along in the early part of this century and, as chairman of the US Fed, drove interest rates down to record lows in order to stimulate the economy after the dot-com bubble burst. It enabled all those sub-prime borrowers to take out mortgages that they subsequently defaulted on. There followed the 2008 crash and, guess what, his successor Ben Bernanke has zeroed prime interest rates indefinitely, or at least until the unemployment rate in America has fallen to 6.5%. The mechanism he uses is to purchase over one trillion dollars of US treasury bonds annually, essentially meaning that the US government does not have to borrow too much from other people (like the Chinese) to cover its deficit and roll over its loans. It can make ends meet with newly printed money as a substitute for savings.

Europe, the UK and Japan have followed suit in implementing the policy of printing money under the euphemism of "quantitative easing". The flipside of the coin is that many savers who used to rely on a safe income from money held on deposit at the bank or invested in the money markets have had to "reach for yield" – another quaint expression which disguises the fact that such action increases the risk of losing the capital in the event of a market downturn. Indeed, the argument is now put forward that if you don't reach for yield, you will definitely lose out in real terms as your after-tax return from bank interest is nowhere near the rate of inflation. The switch to higher yielding (but also higher risk assets) is promoted as a no-brainer.

Of course, the whole bailout episode in Cyprus has added a new dimension to the punishment of savers. Essentially, those with deposits in excess of €100 000 are going to have to cough up between 20 and 30% of their savings in exchange for bank shares which are pretty much worthless. Literally, big savers are overnight being penalised like criminals with no distinction between honest Cypriot entrepreneurs who have made a lifetime success of their businesses and members of the Russian mafia. Cash under the mattress or a secret hoard of gold must now seem a much better option to many of them. These measures can certainly lead to a run on the small banks.

Debt, debt, glorious debt

The net effect of these strange policies is that the world is now drowning in debt. The only governments that have brought down their national debt-to-GDP ratios are probably Ireland and the UK. The US, Europe and Japan are soldiering on with their budget deficits in the hope that it prevents the "Great Recession" becoming the "Great Depression" and somehow recovery will come sooner rather than later. Small businesses and individuals are being urged to borrow again when unserviceable debt was the cause of the last crash. Total debt in the world is now estimated at around $180 trillion versus total equity capital valued at $65 trillion. Put another way, bond markets are nearly three times the size of stock markets. Any significant rise in interest rates triggered by an increase in inflation could thus have a spectacular impact on all markets.

The old and the new thinking

All in all, I would be intrigued to know what my guru Paul Samuelson would have thought of this if he had been alive today. Would he have disagreed with his Nobel-prize winning successor, Paul Krugman, who believes that the creation of new jobs in the US is paramount and nothing in the short term should be done to trim aggregate demand even when it is entirely financed by credit? The new thinking is to kick the can down the road and let renewed economic growth sort the problem out in the longer term. Who am I to argue with Krugman, but justice is not being served when savers are demoted below borrowers.

No easy answers on where to put your money

Oh for the boom that existed between 1982 and 2000, when you could sleep at night as your store of wealth silently multiplied in the stock market and banks were absolutely secure. Now fear has replaced complacency, and for many retirees the future is uncertain.

The one thing the whole Cyprus saga has done is to focus people's attention on where they should store their wealth. According to the latest news, high net worth individuals could lose even more than 30% of their deposits in Cypriot banks and be given pretty worthless bank shares in exchange. That is a serious hit, but I guess it is better than the bank going under and as a depositor your losing everything.

A new precedent

The banking industry relies on trust and if that evaporates, all hell will break loose. Depositors en masse will try to get their money out in order to keep their assets in physical form (gold, property, diamonds, antiques etc.) or in paper form (cash under the mattress, directly held equities/bonds, unit trusts etc.)

Up until now, the retail banking industry has been bailed out as governments are well aware of this worst-case scenario. The financial crash in 2008 meant that many famous retail banks in the US, UK and Europe had to be propped up by government funds in one way or another. In the UK in particular, some of the banks were nationalised and the British government still has a majority equity share in them. New regulations and controls with names like Basel 3 have been enacted in order to boost the capital structure of banks. Moreover, in the UK the regulator will in future have the power to split banks up and separate their retail business from their investment and trading arms in the event of bad behaviour. Recent examples of rogue traders in banks losing anywhere from $2 billion to $6 billion in an undetected series of trades are now at the forefront of legislators' minds.

Yet Cyprus, despite its tiny size in global terms, represents a turning point. Unlike Barings and Lehman Brothers which were principally investment banks that went bust (they did have deposits, but it was not their core business), we now have an example of a major retail bank almost certainly going to the wall. Small depositors are being protected but the large ones are not. The die is now cast and the world is never going to be quite the same again. Any large depositor in a local bank in a small country or even in banks in large countries under financial stress like Italy and Spain must be wondering whether a repeat is possible and withdrawal of funds now is the most sensible strategy. Contagion is the thing policy-makers fear most.

The grass is not always greener on the other side

However, the other investment options for depositors wishing to change the way they handle their money are not necessarily less risky as 2008 has already shown. The majority of hedge funds and exotically named vehicles which were supposed to provide downside protection did not in fact do so in bad times. Their mathematical models proved wrong. Many ordinary unit trusts and umbrella funds have stiff management fees attached to them which have to be paid before you earn a return. Cash under the mattress or gold coins hidden in the garden run the risk of robbery. Property can be a high maintenance asset especially with tricky tenants. You have to know your antiques to buy them profitably.

So the dilemma about where to invest is real which calls

for some innovative thinking. I know that ETFs (exchange-traded funds) have become increasingly popular for all the reasons I have cited plus you know exactly what you are invested in. They are transparent and cheap to administer. Yet stock markets are at or close to all-time highs just as Eurozone unemployment has hit a record 12%. Some of the indices represented by ETFs must at this point be vulnerable to correction, as must be the ETFs tracking commodities and bonds. I have also heard that people are investigating the purchase of digital currencies like bitcoins but they appear to fluctuate in value as much as gold.

Diversification is prudent

With all these variables and uncertainties, the only answer is, if possible, to have a diversified portfolio across a range of asset categories, markets and currencies. Bear in mind that income is just as important as capital gain. Like a fox, keep your eyes open all the time to the changes taking place in the environment in case you have to adapt your strategy and tactics fairly quickly in order to be ahead of the crowd. Don't be greedy and get yourself a trustworthy financial adviser with a good track record. Above all, don't be lulled into making big bets with an excessive amount of your assets. Now is not the time to gamble with your life savings.

Those were the days, my friend

This is one of my most popular online articles. It indicated why it is sometimes more advantageous to publish one's thoughts on the internet than in hard copy. The article went viral here and overseas and I received plenty of supportive emails from people around my age.

We do think alike as we get older.

I saw a beautiful movie recently called *Quartet* featuring four retired opera singers performing together at an old age home for retired musicians. Played by Maggie Smith, Billy Connolly, Tom Courtney and Pauline Collins (whom I remember as Shirley Valentine talking to the wall), the four sing at an annual gala concert held on Verdi's birthday at the home. Of course, they were only play-acting, but they were accompanied by real musicians who had reached the top of their professions in their previous careers.

The democracy of ageing

The film really got to me for two reasons. The first one is that as I get older, everybody gets older with me. No matter how rich you are, no matter how healthy a life you lead, you age. Julia Roberts now has lines on her face, Robert Redford's eyes are even more crinkled and Mick Jagger cannot strut his stuff quite as energetically as he used to. The memory bank grows as the future shortens and the body grows weary.

I spent 11 years going to a British nursing home in Salisbury, Wiltshire to see my mother. As an only child, I would spend two to three weeks with her every year. I remember one evening in the communal dining room sitting at a round table with my mother and some of her co-residents. We were all sipping our regulation one glass of red wine when an old lady at the table says: 'Why are we all here?' Her companion in her late 80s replies: 'Because, my dear, we are not all there!' Logical and very funny and all of us nearly laughed ourselves to death.

Just like the home in the movie, there was a lot of fun and mischief and interesting interplay between the residents and the much younger staff. I thoroughly enjoyed those 11 years and when my mother died a few years ago, I said goodbye to all the people at the home with a genuine heaviness of heart. I haven't been back since, thus it has joined all the other memories in my bank. Yet I know, God willing, that one day through the democratic process of ageing I will be joining those ranks. Nothing can put that off.

The eternity of music

However, there is one thing that does not age and that is the beauty of music and the passion to play it. In their advanced years, those musicians in the film – playing piano, violin, bass and wind instruments – did it with the same gusto as they had done in their prime. Which brings me to the second reason I loved the movie: I was a musician too but not of that elite sort. I played rock music with a friend of mine around the UK in the 1960s and one of my memories (which no one can take away) was playing at the same gig as the Rolling Stones in the summer of 1964. We alternated on the stage all the way through the night and had a big breakfast with all the party-goers in the morning.

The Stones are now celebrating their 50 years together with a concert in Hyde Park. I am sure they will blow the crowd away. In my case, I came out of retirement in the parking lot of the Rosebank shopping mall the other day in Johannesburg. A busker was playing a 1960s song on his guitar at the pay point, so I offered to show him how we played it at the time. I must have been an interesting sight for some of the shoppers who came up to pay, as they did drop coins into his hat.

So I would like to end this chapter by quoting the magnificent lyrics of Gene Raskin, an American folk singer, in a song made famous by Mary Hopkin in 1968:

Those were the days my friend
We thought they'd never end
We'd sing and dance forever and a day
We'd live the life we choose
We'd fight and never lose
For we were young and sure to have our way.

Old age is not for sissies, but it is also a privilege bestowed by surviving the slings and arrows of life. Enjoy it while you can.

The changing nature of work

For me, it is amazing that the teaching profession around the world has not woken up to the facts contained in this article. Schools, universities and other educational institutions are supposed to prepare young people for the world that exists today and not the one that existed 50 years ago. Even business schools have not woken up. They still sideline entrepreneurial training programmes as elective courses well below the status of the MBA.

Foxes scan the environment all the time for red and green flags. A filthy great red flag went up in South Africa in 2013 with the announcement that we lost 100 000 jobs in the first quarter of the year. Our official unemployment rate is just over 25% but on broader criteria could be as high as 40%. Wow! America frets over an unemployment rate north of 7% and is printing dollars to reduce it. In April, the result was an extra 165 000 jobs which reduced the rate to 7.5% that is still unacceptably high by American standards.

We, by contrast, are light years away from that rate and are heading in the wrong direction. So rather than being retrospective and looking for whom and what to blame, let's look at how we can start to resolve the problem in the future bearing in mind that America's record unemployment rate was also 25% when it hit that figure in 1932 during the Great Depression.

Recognising the game has changed

Before foxes decide on the best plan of action, they study the game to see how it has changed – in this case the employment game. Judging from the cover of *The Economist* which had the words "Generation jobless" to indicate the issue of youth unemployment around the world, the change has been radical. The two main sources of employment since the Second World War – the civil service and big business – have now dried up. Governments are having to battle declining tax revenue, budget deficits and an enormous excess of debt and established business is trying to cope with economic hard times worldwide. The only way to grow your business is to take someone else's market share which means having a lower cost base, higher productivity and a greater spirit of innovation. The arrival of management consultants in head offices signals only one thing: retrenchments on a large scale, those left unscathed working like exhausted hamsters, technology replacing people and the CEO taking credit for growing profits against all odds at the next annual general meeting.

Meanwhile, the education system in virtually every country bar Germany is still churning out kids for the job market of the last century: achieve a good mark in your final exam, get a good degree at university, brandish your results to your choice of employers in the public and private sector and you are bound to get a job. Yet, as *The Economist* indicates, the word "job" is rapidly becoming like the word "dinosaur" for aspiring young job seekers. The classic definition covers a dying breed and the latter have never been trained for any alternative. They grow bewildered, then angry and then in some cases like the Arab Spring, revolutionary.

Before getting on to what we have to do to set the ship on the correct course, three further points have to be made:

■ public works programmes do not create permanent jobs. They can teach people new skills but as the new stadiums for the 2010 Soccer World Cup, have shown, when the work is over it's over. Spending R3 trillion to upgrade our infrastructure is a good start but it does not resolve the problem on a long term basis.

■ the logical conclusion of examining the changes in the employment game is that the only real job creator around is small business and ushering in a new generation of entrepreneurs. To create 11 million jobs by 2030 and bring our unemployment rate down to 6% will require the establishment and nurturing of at least another 2 million businesses. That should be our prime target because nothing else can provide a permanent solution.

■ we have to accept we are no longer a frontier economy like all other African economies. They can grow at a rate of 7 to 8% per annum because they have open spaces like the Serengeti for entrepreneurs to do their thing. We, by contrast, ceased to be a frontier economy in the dying moments of the 19th century when first the diamond mines and then the gold mines and then all the service providers to the mines like the banks and the breweries were consolidated into large enterprises. Now we have a crowded economy with little space for entrepreneurs to grow. I will never forget when I was being shown around the Central Party School outside Beijing, which is the leadership academy for the Chinese Communist Party, noticing that in many lecture rooms Chairman Mao's quotations had been replaced by quotes byDeng, his successor. When I asked a professor for the reason, he said that Deng had taught the party to retreat from the economy and allow enough space for local and foreign entrepreneurs to thrive. That was the basis for the Chinese economic miracle.

Winning the game

Given the changing nature of work, what must we do? In previous columns, I have mentioned many of the steps we should take so I will confine myself to the most important ones here:

- We must change our vision from creating new jobs to creating new enterprises with a target of 2 million by 2030. We have 15.5 million citizens on welfare and we should do everything to turn at least 10 to 20% of them into entrepreneurs. They in turn will hire some of the remainder – seven jobs each and you will reach the 11 million NDP job target ahead of time. As Steve Biko said: 'Handouts do not improve your self-esteem: doing it for yourself does.'
- We should have an Economic Codesa as soon as possible where government and the captains of industry produce a blueprint that gives entrepreneurs not only the space they require but also the support in terms of finance, tax incentives, freedom to hire and fire, exemptions from onerous and unnecessary regulations, being part of the supply chain of big business and being paid promptly for the services they provide using the latest smart technologies.
- We need to review our education system to produce young people for the job market of today and not yesterday. Every school should have an entrepreneurial programme to teach pupils how to turn their passions into commercial ideas, how to team up with kindred spirits, how to market themselves and how to make money.

Another uplifting 24 hours in South Africa

Next week, take a notebook with you and note down all the pockets of excellence you encountered in your daily routine. Like birds in the Kruger National Park, you may be surprised by the number of different species you spotted.

Deluged as you are with the bad news of crime and corruption, families landing their relations at the wrong airports and unions fighting one another in the workplace, you can still spend 24 uplifting hours in South Africa. You can still feel that this is a great place to live and you can still marvel at the wonderful and innovative people around you. Of course for that short period of time, you have to block out all the news reports and turn your eyes away from the headlines on newspaper stands and those earnest faces giving you breaking news on the TV screens.

My way of switching into a positive mode is to make a mental note of all the pockets of excellence I have run into during my daily existence here. Recently, I experienced three in 24 hours; one through my ears, the second through my mouth and the third through my feet.

Trust, but verify

My first experience was attending a breakfast at the Fairlawns Boutique Hotel in Johannesburg where I learnt that we are the world's leader in biometric systems used for access control into offices. One in five employees now check in and out using their finger or thumb print, a much higher ratio than in the US. Virtually all the world's leading advances in this field emanate from South Africa. It has huge potential now as a device to protect your internet site and your bank account. Did you know that for every one dollar stolen from American banks using the classical technique of holding up staff with shotguns, over one hundred dollars is stolen using cyber-theft? Fascinating too is that every US President is issued with a "biscuit" which has the nuclear weapons launch code. One completely mislaid it and brazenly denied the fact for weeks to his security detail; and another one sent it to the dry-cleaners.

The point of these stories is that no card and no pin number is directly linked to an individual like a unique fingerprint that you carry around with you all the time. A biometric system not only verifies that it is your fingerprint, it reduces it to an algorithm that cannot be reassembled by hacking into a computer. I know a number of you readers will immediately say that this will only be an added incentive to a robber to cut off your finger; but the new device will be able to measure whether there is a pulse in your finger and distinguish between a live and dead one. Skin grafts are beyond the normal bandit. So, as one of the presenters said, the future no longer lies in your hands but at the tip of your fingers. Incidentally, 90% of the people committing cyber fraud have no previous conviction so profiling is useless.

A spicy opening

After the breakfast, I flew to Durban to give a talk at a function for estate agents and stayed overnight at the Elangeni. The hotel has just opened a steak house on the ground floor and the food was exceptional. I had a fillet cooked to perfection with a genuine Madagascar sauce, big non-greasy chips and spinach that had not been overcooked into an unrecognisable mush. The starter reminded me of Istanbul because it was a spicy, hot spread that you could put on your bread rolls. The point worth making is that although the tab was quite pricey by South African standards, the meal would have cost at least double in Perth or London.

A morning walk

The following morning I went for a walk down the beach front to uShaka Marine World. The promenade they have created beats the beach fronts in Sydney or anywhere in the UK but that is not difficult. The surfers, canoeists, joggers and walkers like me were experiencing the sheer heaven of another day on Earth where nothing can get in the way of the pleasure you feel. There was one police van along the entire strip and no one – not even the many women walking or jogging alone – looked as if they felt insecure. Equally, the place was free of litter and I thought we are world class if only we all try and work together.

From Istanbul with love

After a trip to Turkey in April 2013, I wrote this column. While being bowled over by the entrepreneurial energy on display on every street corner in Istanbul, I had no premonition that the city would become a cauldron of demonstrations against the government within days of leaving. One guide expressed reservations about the current leadership trying to turn the clock back on reforms made by Atatürk but that was it.

As I constantly admit, even with the bright eyes of a fox, one will never anticipate everything that happens. The phrase "out of the blue" was coined for a reason.

If you ever want to enjoy something completely different, go to Istanbul where West meets East over the touchline of the Bosphorus. Apart from all the buildings of great historical interest like the Blue Mosque and the Hagia Sophia, the sheer energy of the city overwhelms you and three words constantly enter your mind: Turks work hard.

Let me give you one example. On my first night there, I went to a small restaurant just up the road from my hotel. The manager not only gives you the menu, he offers a spicy starter for free, gives a glowing history of Turkish beer, harangues his family in the kitchen about what a special customer is sitting at the table and the food must be prepared with the utmost care and finally dives outside to solicit passing tourists to come into his personalised eating place. I joined him in the street after being fortified by his Turkish coffee and we managed to persuade some Australians to give his restaurant a shot.

But that is Istanbul. Everywhere you go there are entrepreneurs seeking to make a living out of the 11 million tourists that visit the city each year and the 35 million tourists that come to the country as a whole. The streets, particularly in the old Western section, are one long line of small service providers from mending the chains the boats use to anchor themselves to rows of do-it-yourself shops selling every household gadget you can imagine to orange squeezers quenching the thirst of pedestrians as they pass by with the cups being disposed in a bin attached to the stall.

In two places, the entrepreneurial frenzy reaches a peak: the Grand Bazaar and the Spice Market. Both are covered malls of one level with a constant river of people flowing through them, mainly curious tourists wanting to get a good bargain to show their family and friends back home. Overlooking this moving mass is one man whose photograph appears on the walls of all the buildings you pass through: Mustafa Kemal Atatürk. He is the Nelson Mandela of Turkey, having founded the modern Turkish state in the 1920s and established a secular society where Islam and the economy are balanced against one another. It is a model which has led Turkey to an annual income per head of $10 000 for its 80 million citizens. Ironically, Turkey has knocked on the door of the European Union for a few decades now but has been denied membership. Now the tables are turned and Turks look on their Western neighbours, particularly the Greeks with whom they have always shared a rivalry, with a mixture of pity and amusement.

The message for us in South Africa from Istanbul is simple. If we are to create an inclusive economy in which all our citizens participate to create a better life for themselves, then we need to develop the space for millions of small businesses to ply their trade side by side. All our major cities should have their equivalent of the Grand Bazaar attracting a steady stream of local and foreign customers; but you also need a network of alleys of small shops you can explore. Above all we need to work hard.

God's messy war

Throughout the history of mankind, religion may have given individuals internal peace but it has been responsible for many wars. The Middle East remains at the epicentre of this tendency.

Three developments suggest that God's messy war has no end in sight and could get worse.

Firstly, the Boston bombings indicate that self-radicalisation – a term to denote an individual's conversion from religious zealotry to acts of violence – is on the increase. From an intelligence point of view, this turn of events is potentially very dangerous as it is almost impossible to pick up the signs of a specific individual taking the leap from abstract idea to ghastly deed; and the measures required to reduce the probability of this scenario become extremely costly in terms of money and denial of freedoms which are the foundation of democracy. The butchering of a soldier in civvies in broad daylight in Woolwich in London and impromptu statements by one of his attackers holding a bloody knife and cleaver have increased the urgency of new tactics to counter this trend; as has the incident of a soldier in uniform being almost killed in Paris by being stabbed in the neck.

Secondly, the public acknowledgement by President Obama of the use of drones to kill the leadership of terrorist movements in countries like Pakistan and Yemen indicates how much the game of war has changed. Some three thousand people have been killed, including around 10% of that number being innocent civilians who are described as collateral damage. As I said in a previous column, conventional forces such as armies, navies and airforces become redundant in such a war. It's all about a model aeroplane being directed by a computer boffin sitting in an office in some unknown location in America. With the withdrawal of British and American troops from Afghanistan in 2014, this will become the principal tactic of the West in the overseas fight against terrorism in the years to come. Clinical and remote and maybe joined by robots in time.

Thirdly, the civil war in Syria between rival groups of the same religious faith has just escalated to a new level with the announcement by the Russians that they are supplying the latest anti-aircraft missiles to the Syrian government forces. The war there is already threatening to engulf neighbouring states like Turkey, Lebanon and Israel; and the declared willingness of Britain and France to arm the rebels can only lead to a greater intensity of the battle inside Syria itself. Iraq is also a warzone again between rival religious factions.

There are a host of reasons why wars in history have broken out ranging from emperors wanting to expand their sway in Roman times, the crusades, the historical rivalry between European and other nations and the sheer hatred between different ethnic groups causing genocide in different parts of the world. Then there are the revolutions around ideology or precipitated by the more materialistic ambitions of grabbing power and becoming the next elite in a particular country. The killing will continue as it is in the basic DNA of mankind to compete and fight with intervals of peace breaking out when exhaustion sets in. Religion seems to be the latest excuse to fight but it is the hardest one to quell. Tolerance is the exception rather than the rule when it comes to matters of God.

The Born Frees

I wish more South African politicians would have town hall meetings with students to understand what really makes them tick.

At a breakfast this week, I was introduced to a new term the "Born Frees", being all those young people who were born in 1994 or thereafter in South Africa. The man who introduced me to this phrase was interested to know my opinion on who these Born Frees would vote for in the next election. The point was that this would be the first election in which these young people could vote.

The great divide

My answer was non-committal as I do not think either of the two major parties in this country – the ANC and the DA – really offer much of substance to the Born Frees. The youth wing of the ANC have gone into a free fall ever since Julius Malema was expelled and are now up to their ears in debt. Whatever you may say about Julius, he did have and probably still does have a considerable following among young people who feel economically disenfranchised. No young star has emerged in the ANC to fill his boots and wow the audiences like Julius did. Essentially the leadership of the ruling party is now a middle-aged and elderly bunch in the eyes of the Born Frees – more like Rodriguez than Justin Bieber.

As for the DA, nobody has emerged with the ability of Julius to have the crowds dancing and cheering and lapping up every word. There are some brilliant young intellectuals in the DA, but they do not possess the charisma necessary to swing the vote of the Born Frees in the DA's favour. All the other minority parties are led by the people of the same generation as the ANC. Yes, they do have some bright ideas about improving the prospects of young South Africans but they are not going to rock them in the aisle.

Consequently, there is a vacuum in the political arena. Even on the economic side the National Development Plan has failed to make a significant dent in the imagination of the vast majority of youth in their late teens and early twenties. I doubt whether many of them have read the voluminous document and nobody in the National Planning Commission has tried to turn it into a popular treatise or DVD topping the local charts. Maybe even a rap song is needed, highlighting the positives to a hypnotic beat and possessing a chorus line that everybody will remember when downloading it from YouTube. If Psy can do it with Gangnam Style , so can Trevor or Cyril.

Meet the young lions and lionesses

Meanwhile, I have had one experience of the Born Frees en masse this year. It was a meeting of the Investment Society at UCT in Jammie Hall. Being held in the evening, I thought a couple of dozen students would pitch up to the event – instead of which the hall was packed to capacity with not one member of the faculty being evident in the room. I talked about entrepreneurship, economic freedom and doing your own thing as the boss of your own small business as opposed to slaving away in some big company, the civil service or as a junior functionary in a public works programme. They gave me a standing ovation at the end when I said "for fox sake, let's make it happen".

Since then I have come across two projects which reflect the spirit of the new generation of Born Frees. The first is a partnership between Goldman Sachs and GIBS to empower young women to become successful entrepreneurs. As long as you as a member of the fairer sex have been in business for a year and have an annual turnover of between R200 000 and R7m and are located in Gauteng, Polokwane, North West Province or Mpumalanga, you can qualify for the programme.

The second initiative was celebrated at the breakfast I talked about at the beginning of the article: The Hope Factory which with the backing of the South African Institute of Chartered Accountants has equipped 300 grassroots entrepreneurs to make it through the survivalist, subsistence phase and move towards becoming a sustainable small business and maybe a large corporate one day. I could mention many other projects as well.

The bottom line is that the Born Frees do not want hand-outs from the state, do not want to be slaves in some vast organisation and do not want to be fed the same old political and economic myths that their parents fell for. They do not want to walk behind anyone, they want to walk in front – creating their own future for themselves. It is our job as the older generation to provide the environment which allows those dreams to be fulfilled.

The foresight of Eric Arthur Blair

It is not often that a Wykehamist has good words to say about an old Etonian but this one was exceptional.

He described himself as lower-upper-middle class, but went to the poshest school in England – Eton College. He suffered ill-health most of his life, but volunteered to fight and saw action in the Spanish Civil War. He lived like a tramp in London and Paris, but represented the British Empire as a policeman in Burma. He regularly attended holy communion but was one of the most cynical writers about human nature. Consider these three quotes: 'Power is tearing human minds apart and putting them back together in new shapes of your own choosing.' 'One does not establish a dictatorship in order to safeguard a revolution; one makes a revolution in order to establish a dictatorship.' 'If you want a picture of the future, imagine a boot stamping on a human face – forever.'

He died of TB at the age of 46 on a chilly morning in January 1950, and his gravestone in All Saints' Churchyard in Oxfordshire has the brief epitaph: 'Here lies Eric Arthur Blair, born 25 June 1903, died 21 January 1950.' His life was a glorious contradiction but he did make the following admission: 'Doublethink means the power of holding two contradictory beliefs in one's mind simultaneously, and accepting both of them.' So now I can reveal his pen name, George Orwell, inventor of phrases like "the thought police" and "thoughtcrimes". He wrote *Animal Farm* in 1945 and published *1984* in 1949 just before his death. His two most famous sayings are: 'All animals are equal, but some animals are more equal than others' and 'Big Brother is watching you'.

As a scenario planner, I have to bow in front of a man who had such extraordinary powers of prophecy. The first book captured the nature of communist dictatorships around the world in the second half of the last century. I love the excerpt: 'The creatures outside looked from pig to man, and from man to pig, and from pig to man again; but already it was impossible to say which was which.' Equally, the quip that 'Man serves the interests of no creature but himself' anticipates the wanton destruction of the natural environment around us in pursuit of wealth.

Yet, the second book is the real masterpiece because it is a completely accurate precursor of the latest newspaper scoop on intelligence agencies hoovering up all our e-mails and telephone records. No wonder that Amazon has virtually run out of copies of *1984* on account of the sudden leap in demand. It is called a "dystopian novel" because it describes a place where everything is as bad as it can be. We now live in an Orwellian world where privacy no longer exists and our every communication is scrutinised to see if we are "a person of interest". God forbid that we become one as that is when life can become very nasty indeed. As Orwell himself said: 'If you want a secret, you must also hide it from yourself.'

Poised on a knife-edge

The US economy is now showing signs of recovery. Is it sustainable when the era of cheap money ends? Or will the law of unintended consequences create another crash?

I am so glad David Shapiro, a leading commentator on stock markets, agreed on the radio with a point I made in an article some time ago: Ben Bernanke is the most powerful person in the world as Chairman of the US Federal Reserve, even more powerful than Barack Obama because his words can shift markets all over the world.

As I said: 'Bernanke has zeroed interest rates to stimulate recovery . . . if he has got the balance right the US economy will gradually recover . . . if he has overcooked the brew, central banks around the world will start showing enormous losses on their holdings of US treasuries. Whereas the first financial crisis this century was related to commercial banks, the second one will centre on central banks with much more devastating consequences.'

Bernanke is walking a fine line. He was quite upbeat about prospects for the US economy in terms of future growth and the unemployment rate falling in the next two years to 6.5% from its current 7.6%. However, while hedging his bets by saying that he would keep all his options open as the figures rolled in, he intimated that the Fed's monthly programme of buying $85bn of mortgage bonds and treasuries might be tapered down later this year and end in 2014. Boom! The Dow Jones Industrial Average fell 1.35% on this news as much of the US stock market's strength recently has been due to zero interest rates driving people to take their money out of the bank and invest it in shares yielding a higher return. This flow could of course reverse if interest rates now start to rise on the expectation that the Fed's artificial stimulus is about to be curbed. Then the bond bubble could burst causing further chaos.

The best metaphor to describe the current situation is to liken the US economy to a patient in ICU. Doctor Ben is betting on the patient now being in a recovery mode such that the tube pumping zero interest rate fluid into the veins is no longer as critical as it was and can gradually be removed. Eventually, the patient will return to normal and be self-sustaining. The stock market, on the other hand, is hooked on the tube remaining in place for much longer and maybe forever. The bulls like the adrenalin rush caused by easy money and they do not want it to end, whatever happens in the real economy. The bears feel that the patient's vital signs, as seen in the regular blips on the heart monitor, may disappear into a flat line following any reduction in dosage. In a funny way, therefore, they both agree that Doctor Ben should carry on without making any suggestion that a change in regimen is in the offing. That proposition spooks everyone.

I cannot tell you who is right and who is wrong about the patient's condition at this moment in time. Can we trust the doctor or not? Nevertheless, we are reaching a moment of truth where Bernanke is either shown to have been a man of great wisdom in pulling off one of the greatest monetary miracles of all time, or he is shown to have learnt nothing from the failures of his predecessor, Alan Greenspan, who also followed the policy of cheap money but cut off the drip too soon in 2007. Worse still, the drip may be the source of the problem as it offered an easy way out and stopped the patient from reforming his unhealthy lifestyle!

Cool Namibia

In South Africa, we must have the humility to learn from other countries in Africa – in this instance Namibia.

A while back I flew to Windhoek to be a guest speaker at an awards dinner arranged for the first time by the Namibian Manufacturers Association. I felt quite chuffed because the other South African performing at the same function was Khaya Mthetwa, our 2012 winner of *Idols*. We had a chat before the dinner and it was clear that one of the reasons he won the title was the age-old formula of passion plus homework to succeed in your occupation. He really sweated the small stuff to stay ahead of his competitors – and he has a great voice too.

However, the reason for this article is that whenever I go to Namibia, I come back with a mixture of tranquillity, joy and renewed hope that we in South Africa can get it right too. Black Namibian citizens get on with German citizens who get on with Afrikaans citizens and everybody else comes along for the ride. Namibia gained independence only a few years ahead of us, yet they seem to have settled down to getting on with life and hopefully raising the quality of it for all their citizenry.

Yes, it is a small country with only 2.3 million inhabitants and yes it has the same level of youth unemployment of just over 50% that we have. But somehow people are not nearly as angry and combative as they are here. Quite a few senior South African business executives seconded to posts in their companies in Namibia privately expressed their wish to stay beyond their period of secondment. Their stated reason was that people are so nice and friendly, everybody works as a team, the media does not offer a daily dose of hate stories, the violent crime rate is much lower and even the SWAPO youth wing leader apologised publicly for some of the comments he had made.

Now I know that some of you reading this book will say that Windhoek does not represent the country. I fully understand that as I did a road show around the entire country for a bank several years ago and there are deep pockets of poverty as you go to the extreme north. Yet a peacefulness reigns. Namibians may be poorer than us, have less mineral riches and have a sparse natural environment but they probably rank higher on the happiness index. Moreover, Namibia's economic growth rate in 2012 was 5%, exactly double our figure of 2.5%.

David Moseley's observation on the ugly conduct of South Africans towards parking officials and students selling match programmes is not evident on the streets of Windhoek where courteous behaviour is shown even to the humblest individual trying to ply his or her trade. At the awards dinner, the final speaker was the Honourable Calle Schlettwein, Minister of Trade and Industry. He outlined the "growth at home" programme which has objectives broadly in line with our National Development Plan, namely to accelerate economic growth, reduce income inequality and increase employment. Good luck to him. He quoted Henry Ford: 'Coming together is a beginning; keeping together is progress; working together is success.'

Consistent with this theme, Khaya sang a song in his cabaret with all the verve of the original artist, Otis Redding. It is entitled "Try a little tenderness" and includes the lines 'Hey, hey you gotta know what to do, don't be a fool, you need to try it now.'

Of course, in the case of Namibia, the occupier – South Africa – left when that country gained true independence. We in South Africa face the more daunting task of seeking reconciliation between all the people who were and still are here. Maybe, we have got to try a bit harder in South Africa to replicate the coolness of Namibians. But we must chill out a bit as well and just get on with it.

The world of natural knocks

I am sorry to end this book with such a stark warning. However, it corroborates the eighth megatrend of the opening article. Climate change poses the biggest threat of all to our future because nobody outside the environmental field perceives it as a threat. Weather of any kind is just taken for granted. Please don't do that any more. All you have to do is ask the citizens of the Philippines how they feel after the terrible loss of life and damage to property that they suffered from the record-breaking storm that hit their islands. It should be on the conscience of the super-emitters of carbon dioxide that they are partially responsible for this tragedy and it will be a case of gross negligence if they do not do something to curb their emission of greenhouse gases.

A popular expression is that you have got to where you are today because of going to the school of hard knocks. In other words, experience has moulded your character and contributed to your learning. The teachers did the academic part and the world did the rest.

Alas, this principle does not apply to improving our environmental awareness. 2013 has seen a world of spectacular natural knocks and we are not even debating what we are going to do about it. On CNN, the weatherman said that people in California must, wherever possible, drink water and carry it around with them so that they do not suffer dehydration in the excessive temperatures this state is experiencing. In parts of California, temperatures are expected to hover around or even exceed 50 °C. The map was covered with deep purple over the west coast of America. Meanwhile, he also warned that from Florida to New England on the east coast heavy and drenching rains were expected. All this came days after the tragedy of 19 firefighters from the best tactical unit in Arizona being killed in a gigantic fire as a result of high winds changing direction.

2013 has been a horrible year so far. I wrote a previous article on how the interior of Australia might become un-inhabitable because of the record high temperatures reached there at the beginning of the year. European cities on major rivers have had terrible flooding and so has Calgary in western Canada. India and China, which admittedly have annual battles against extreme weather, yet again are going through the throes of having to rescue hundreds of thousands of people from rising waters. America itself has had super tornadoes making towns look as if an atomic bomb has been dropped on them.

As a scenario planner, and a foxy one at that, I feel the flags are going up everywhere to indicate a major change in climate meriting examination and appropriate action. I know that global warming has been on the radar system for a long time and we have major summits every four years. But somehow you get the impression that this issue is not being addressed with the seriousness it deserves. If terrorists had caused the damage the weather has this year, the world would be up in arms, the media would have screaming headlines and G8, G20 and the UN would be meeting every week to resolve the problem. Drastic action would have already been taken.

I know that the naysayers on climate change will have a field day with what I have said and continue to describe the whole theory as a conspiracy. They will argue that the natural knocks I am talking about have always been around.

I also know that another group will argue that I am missing the point and actually the whole thing comes down to over-population of the planet. Furthermore, here we are trying to recover from the Great Recession and the last thing we need to do is go off at a tangent – that will be the retort of many political leaders.

All I can say in response is that I am not by profession an environmentalist and I do not have special axes to grind. I spent my life in business and I can see a catastrophe in the making for our children and grandchildren if we do not act now.